BULTMANN

OUTSTANDING CHRISTIAN THINKERS

Series Editor: Brian Davies OP

The series offers a range of authoritative studies on people who have made an outstanding contribution to Christian thought and understanding. The series will range across the full spectrum of Christian thought to include Catholic and Protestant thinkers, to cover East and West, historical and contemporary figures. By and large, each volume will focus on a single 'thinker', but occasionally the subject may be a movement or a school of thought.

Brian Davies, OP, the Series Editor, is Regent of Studies at Blackfriars, Oxford, where he also teaches philosophy. He is a member of the Theology Faculty at the University of Oxford and tutor at St Benet's Hall, Oxford. He has lectured regularly at the University of Bristol, Fordham University, New York, and the Beda College, Rome. He is Reviews Editor of *New Blackfriars*. His previous publications include: *An Introduction to the Philosophy of Religion* (OUP, 1982); *Thinking about God* (Geoffrey Chapman, 1985); *The Thought of Thomas Aquinas* (OUP, 1992); and he was editor of *Language, Meaning and God* (Geoffrey Chapman, 1987).

Already published:

The Apostolic Fathers
Simon Tugwell OP

Denys the Areopagite
Andrew Louth

The Venerable Bede
Benedicta Ward SLG

Anselm
G. R. Evans

Teresa of Avila
Rowan Williams

Handel
Hamish Swanston

Bultmann
David Fergusson

Reinhold Niebuhr
Kenneth Durkin

Yves Congar
Aidan Nichols OP

Planned titles in the series include:

Karl Rahner
William V. Dych SJ

Lonergan
Frederick E. Crowe SJ

Hans Urs von Balthasar
John O'Donnell SJ

BULTMANN

David Fergusson

A Michael Glazier Book
THE LITURGICAL PRESS
Collegeville, Minnesota

A Michael Glazier Book
published by The Liturgical Press
St John's Abbey, Collegeville, MN 56321, USA

© David A. Fergusson 1992

Published in Great Britain by Geoffrey Chapman, an imprint of
Cassell Publishers Limited

First published 1992

Library of Congress Cataloging-in-Publication Data
A catalog record for this book is available from the Library of Congress.

ISBN 0–8146–5037–6

Typeset by Colset Private Limited, Singapore
Printed and bound in Great Britain by
Biddles Ltd, Guildford and King's Lynn

Contents

Editorial foreword

St Anselm of Canterbury once described himself as someone with faith seeking understanding. In words addressed to God he says 'I long to understand in some degree thy truth, which my heart believes and loves. For I do not seek to understand that I may believe, but I believe in order to understand.'

And this is what Christians have always inevitably said, either explicitly or implicitly. Christianity rests on faith, but it also has content. It teaches and proclaims a distinctive and challenging view of reality. It naturally encourages reflection. It is something to think about; something about which one might even have second thoughts.

But what have the greatest Christian thinkers said? And is it worth saying? Does it engage with modern problems? Does it provide us with a vision to live by? Does it make sense? Can it be preached? Is it believable?

This series originates with questions like these in mind. Written by experts, it aims to provide clear, authoritative and critical accounts of outstanding Christian writers from New Testament times to the present. It will range across the full spectrum of Christian thought to include Catholic and Protestant thinkers, thinkers from East and West, thinkers ancient, mediaeval and modern.

The series draws on the best scholarship currently available; so it will interest all with a professional concern for the history of Christian ideas. But contributors will also be writing for general readers who have little or no previous knowledge of the subjects to be dealt with. Volumes to appear should therefore prove helpful at a popular as well as an academic level. For the most part they will be devoted to a single thinker, but occasionally the subject will be a movement or school of thought.

Professor Fergusson's book on Rudolf Bultmann brings us to one of the theological giants of the twentieth century. Bultmann's voluminous and wide-ranging writings have shaped the concerns and methods of several generations of theologians. They are still influential and still much studied, covering, as they do, central issues in systematic theology, biblical criticism, history, philosophy and hermeneutics.

As well as providing an extremely clear and comprehensive overview of Bultmann's career, ideas and impact, Professor Fergusson also shows how his writings form a complex unity. In addition, he indicates how we may critically react to them as theology moves into the twenty-first century. His balance of narrative, exposition, and comment makes his book admirably suited to the needs of all readers who want to know what Bultmann thought, and what they might think of this themselves.

Brian Davies OP

Preface

My interest in Rudolf Bultmann dates back to a course of under-graduate lectures delivered by Elizabeth Templeton at New College, Edinburgh, in 1979. The fusion of faith and modernity in his work has always intrigued me, and, over the years, I have come to appreciate the richness and unity of his theology, biblical criticism and preaching. The range of Bultmann's writings often entails the critic working outside his or her immediate field of expertise. For this reason amongst others, I must record my gratitude to teachers, colleagues and friends whose advice and reading suggestions have assisted me in numerous ways. In particular, I am indebted to Robert Morgan, Douglas Templeton, David Mealand, Bruce McCormack, Wilhelm Hüffmeier and the late Hans Frei.

The major portion of this book was written during a transitional period in which we moved from Edinburgh to Aberdeen. I am indebted to my wife for bearing more than her fair share of domestic responsibilities at this time. We have come to appreciate a little of what Barth felt in 1925 when he wrote to Bultmann that he was tired of buying and selling houses and would soon have enough experience to become an estate agent (*Letters*, p. 25).

Bibliography

Works

An extensive bibliography of the works of Bultmann until 1965 is available in C. W. Kegley (ed.), *The Theology of Rudolf Bultmann* (London, 1966). The following publications are referred to in the course of this study. Titles are listed chronologically with details of republication and English translation where applicable.

Der Stil der paulinischen Predigt und die kynisch-stoische Diatribe (1910 dissertation; Göttingen, 1984).

Die Exegese des Theodor von Mopsuestia (1912 Habilitationsschrift; Stuttgart, 1984).

'Ethische und mystische Religion im Urchristentum', *Die Christliche Welt* (1920), pp. 725–31, 738–43: repr. in J. Moltmann (ed.), *Anfänge der dialektischen Theologie* II (Munich 1967), pp. 29–47; 'Ethical and mystical religion in primitive Christianity' in J. Robinson (ed.), *The Beginnings of Dialectical Theology* (Richmond, 1968), pp. 221–35.

Die Geschichte der synoptischen Tradition (Göttingen, 1921); *The History of the Synoptic Tradition* (London, 1972).

'Karl Barth's Römerbrief in zweiter Auflage', *Die Christliche Welt* (1922), pp. 320–3, 330–4; repr. in J. Moltmann (ed.), *Anfänge der dialektischen Theologie* I (Munich, 1966), pp. 119ff.; 'Review of Barth's Romans' in *Beginnings of Dialectical Theology*, pp. 100–20.

'Die liberale Theologie und die jüngste theologische Bewegung', *Theologische Blätter* (1924), pp. 73–86; repr. GV I, pp. 1–25; 'Liberal theology and the latest theological movement', FU, pp. 28–52.

'Das Problem der Ethik bei Paulus', *Zeitschrift für die neutestamentlische Wissenschaft* (1924), pp. 123–40; repr. Ex, pp. 36–54.

'Die Bedeutung der neuerschlossenen mandäischen und manichäischen Quellen für das Verständnis des Johannesevangeliums', *Zeitschrift für die neutestamentliche Wissenschaft* (1925), pp. 100–46; repr. Ex, pp. 55–104.

'Das Problem einer theologischen Exegese des Neuen Testaments', *Zwischen den Zeiten* (1925), pp. 334–57; repr. in *Anfänge der dialektischen Theologie* II, pp. 47–72; 'The problem of a theological exegesis of the New Testament' in *Beginnings of Dialectical Theology*, pp. 236–56.

'Welchen Sinn hat es, von Gott zu reden?', *Theologische Blätter* (1925), pp. 129–35; repr. GV I, pp. 26–37; 'What does it mean to speak of God?', FU, pp. 53–65.

Jesus (Berlin, 1926); *Jesus and the Word* (London, 1934).

'The new approach to the synoptic problem', *Journal of Religion* (1926), pp. 337–62; EF, pp. 39–62.

'Zur Frage der Christologie', *Zwischen den Zeiten* (1927), pp. 41–69; repr. GV I, pp. 85–113; 'On the question of Christology', FU, pp. 116–44.

'Vom Begriff der religiösen Gemeinschaft', *Theologische Blätter* (1927), pp. 66–73.

'Die Eschatologie des Johannesevangelium', *Zeitschrift für die neutestamentliche Wissenschaft* (1928), pp. 4–22; repr. GV I, pp. 134–52; 'The eschatology of the gospel of John', FU, pp. 165–83.

Der Begriff der Offenbarung im Neuen Testament (Tübingen, 1929); repr. GV III, pp. 1–34; 'The concept of revelation in the New Testament', EF, pp. 67–106.

'Die Geschichtlichkeit des Daseins und der Glaube', *Zeitschrift für Theologie und Kirche* (1930), pp. 329–64; 'The historicity of man and faith', EF, pp. 107–29.

'Paulus' in *Religion in Geschichte und Gegenwart* (Tübingen, 1930), pp. 1019–45; 'Paul', EF, pp. 130–72.

'Die Krisis des Glaubens' in R. Bultmann, H. von Soden and H.

Frick, *Krisis des Glaubens, Krisis der Kirche, Krisis der Religion: Drei Marburger Vorträge* (Marburg, 1931), pp. 5–21; repr. GV II, pp. 1–19; 'The crisis of belief', EPT, pp. 1–21.

'ginōskō' in *Theologisches Wörterbuch zum Neuen Testament* (1933), pp. 688–719; *Gnosis* (London, 1953).

Glauben und Verstehen. Gesammelte Aufsätze I–IV (Tübingen, 1933–65).

'Die Bedeutung des Alten Testaments für den christlichen Glauben', GV I, pp. 313–36; 'The meaning of the Old Testament for Christian faith' in B.W. Anderson (ed.), *The Old Testament and Christian Faith* (London, 1964), pp. 8–35.

'Die Aufgabe der Theologie in der gegenwärtigen Situation', *Theologische Blätter* (1933), pp. 161–6; 'The task of theology in the present situation', EF, pp. 186–95.

'Der Arier-Paragraph im Raume der Kirche', *Theologische Blätter* (1933), pp. 359–70.

'Jesus und Paulus' in *Jesus Christus im Zeugnis der Heil. Schrift und der Kirche* (Munich, 1936), pp. 68–90; 'Jesus and Paul', EF, pp. 217–39.

Christus des Gesetzes Ende (Munich, 1940); repr. GV II, pp. 32–58; 'Christ the end of the law', EPT, pp. 36–66.

Das Evangelium des Johannes (Göttingen, 1941); *The Gospel of John* (Oxford, 1971).

'Neues Testament und Mythologie' in *Offenbarung und Heilsgeschehen* (Munich, 1941); repr. as *Neues Testament und Mythologie*, ed. E. Jüngel (Munich, 1988); 'The New Testament and mythology', K & M, pp. 1–44; NTM, pp. 1–44.

'Die Frage der natürlichen Offenbarung' in *Offenbarung und Heilsgeschehen*; repr. GV II, pp. 79–104; 'The question of natural revelation', EPT, pp. 90–118.

'Anknüpfung und Widerspruch', *Theologische Zeitschrift* (1946), pp. 401–18; repr. GV II, pp. 117–32; 'Points of contact and conflict', EPT, pp. 133–50.

Theologie des Neuen Testaments I–II (Tübingen, 1948–51); *Theology of the New Testament* I–II (London, 1951–55).

'Humanismus und Christentum', *Studium Generale* I (1948),

pp. 70–7; repr. GV II, pp. 133–49; 'Humanism and Christianity', EPT, pp. 151–67.

'Gnade und Freiheit', *Glaube und Geschichte. Festschrift für F. Gogarten* (1948), pp. 7–20; repr. GV II, pp. 149–61; 'Grace and freedom', EPT, pp. 168–81.

Das Urchristentum im Rahmen der antiken Religionen (Zürich, 1949); *Primitive Christianity in its Contemporary Setting* (London, 1957).

'Das Problem der Hermeneutik', *Zeitschrift für Theologie und Kirche* (1950), pp. 47–69; repr. GV II, pp. 211–35; 'The problem of hermeneutics', EPT, pp. 234–61; NTM, pp. 69–94.

'Das christologische Bekenntnis des Ökumenischen Rates', *Schweizerische Theologische Umschau*, xxi (1951), pp. 25–36; repr. GV II, pp. 246–61; 'The Christological confession of the World Council of Churches', EPT, pp. 273–90.

'Zum Problem der Entmythologisierung', KuM II, pp. 177–208; 'On the problem of demythologising', NTM, pp. 95–130.

'Antwort an Karl Jaspers', *Theologische Zeitschrift* (1954), pp. 81–95; repr. KuM III, pp. 47–59.

Die Frage der Entmythologisierung (Munich, 1954); 'The case for demythologising', K & M II, pp. 181–94.

Essays, Philosophical and Theological (London, 1955). Translation of GV II.

Marburger Predigten (Tübingen, 1956); *This World and the Beyond* (London, 1960).

'Ist voraussetzungslose Exegese möglich?', *Theologische Zeitschrift* 13 (1957), pp. 409–17; repr. GV III, pp. 142–50; 'Is exegesis without presuppositions possible?', EF, pp. 342–52; NTM, pp. 145–54.

History and Eschatology (Edinburgh, 1957)/*The Presence of Eternity* (New York, 1957); *Geschichte und Eschatologie* (Tübingen, 1958).

Jesus Christ and Mythology (New York, 1958).

'Gedanken über die gegenwärtige theologische Situation', *The Christian Century* (1958), pp. 967–9; repr. GV III, pp. 190–6.

'Milestones in books', *Expository Times* 70 (1958), p. 125.

Das Verhältnis der urchristlichen Christusbotschaft zum historischen Jesus (Heidelberg, 1960); repr. Ex, pp. 445-69; 'The primitive Christian kerygma and the historical Jesus' in C.E. Braaten and R.A. Harrisville (eds), *The Historical Jesus and the Kerygmatic Christ* (New York, 1964).

Existence and Faith (Shorter Writings of Rudolf Bultmann), ed. S. Ogden (Fontana Library; London, 1964).

'Review of Schubert Ogden, *Christ Without Myth*', *Journal of Religion* 81 (1962), pp. 225-7.

'Ist der Glaube an Gott erledigt?', *Die Zeit* (10 May 1963); repr. GV IV, pp. 107-12; J.A.T. Robinson and D.L. Edwards (eds), *The Honest To God Debate* (London, 1965), pp. 134-8.

'*dikaiosynē Theou*', *Journal of Biblical Literature* 83 (1964), pp. 12-16; repr. Ex, pp. 470-5.

'Reply' in C.W. Kegley (ed.), *The Theology of Rudolf Bultmann* (London, 1966), pp. 257-87.

Exegetica (Tübingen, 1967).

Faith and Understanding (London, 1969). Translation of GV I.

Karl Barth–Rudolf Bultmann: Briefwechsel, 1922-1966, ed. B. Jaspert (vol. 1 of the Karl Barth *Gesamtausgabe*; Zürich, 1971); *Karl Barth–Rudolf Bultmann: Letters, 1922-66* (Edinburgh, 1982).

Theologische Enzyklopädie (Tübingen, 1984).

Das Verkündigte Wort (Tübingen, 1984).

'Theologie als Wissenschaft', *Zeitschrift für Theologie und Kirche*, 81 (1984), pp. 447-69; 'Theology as science', NTM, pp. 45-68.

New Testament and Mythology and Other Basic Writings, ed. S. Ogden (London, 1985).

Secondary works cited

T.W. Adorno, *The Jargon of Authenticity* (London, 1973).

B.W. Anderson, *The Old Testament and Christian Faith* (London, 1964).

D.M. Baillie, *God Was in Christ* (London, 1948).

I.G. Barbour, *Myths, Models and Paradigms* (London, 1974).

BIBLIOGRAPHY

R.S. Barbour, *Traditio-Historical Criticism of the Gospels* (London, 1972).

Karl Barth, *The Epistle to the Romans* (2nd ed., trans. E. Hoskyns; Oxford, 1933).

Church Dogmatics I/1, I/2, III/2, IV/3 (Edinburgh, 1956–62).

'Rudolf Bultmann—an attempt to understand him', K & M II, pp. 83–132.

C.K. Barrett, *The Gospel According to St. John* (2nd ed., London, 1978).

H.W. Bartsch (ed.), *Kerygma und Mythos* I–III (Hamburg, 1948–54); sel. trans. in *Kerygma and Myth* I–II (London, 1962–4).

M. Beintker, *Die Gottesfrage in der Theologie Wilhelm Herrmanns* (Berlin, 1976).

E. Bethge, *Dietrich Bonhoeffer* (London, 1970).

J.M. Bonino, *Revolutionary Theology Comes of Age* (London, 1975).

G. Bornkamm, *Jesus of Nazareth* (London, 1960).

Paul (New York, 1971).

W. Bousset, *Die Religion des Judentums in späthellenistischen Zeitalter* (1926).

C.E. Braaten and R.A. Harrisville (eds), *The Historical Jesus and the Kerygmatic Christ* (Nashville, 1964).

E. Brunner, *The Christian Doctrine of Creation and Redemption* (London, 1952).

A. Bultmann Lemke, 'Der unveröffentliche Nachlass von Rudolf Bultmann' in B. Jaspert (ed.), *Rudolf Bultmanns Werk und Wirkung* (Darmstadt, 1984), pp. 194–207.

'Bultmann's papers' in E.C. Hobbs (ed.), *Bultmann: Retrospect and Prospect* (Philadelphia, 1985), pp. 3–12.

F. Buri, 'Entmythologisierung oder Entkerygmatisierung der Theologie' in *Kerygma und Mythos* II (Hamburg, 1952), pp. 85–101.

D. Cairns, *A Gospel Without Myth* (London, 1960).

S. Coakley, *Christ Without Absolutes* (Oxford, 1988).

A.C. Cochrane, *The Church's Confession under Hitler* (Pittsburgh, 1976).

N. Dahl, 'The problem of the historical Jesus' in C.E. Braaten and R.A. Harrisville (eds), *Kerygma and History* (New York, 1962).

C.H. Dodd, *The Interpretation of the Fourth Gospel* (Cambridge, 1953).

T. Eagleton, *Literary Theory* (Oxford, 1983).

G. Ebeling, *Theology and Proclamation* (London, 1966).

'Word of God and hermeneutics' in *Word and Faith* (London, 1963).

'Zum Verständnis von R. Bultmanns Aufsatz: "Welchen Sinn hat es, von Gott zu reden?" ' in *Wort und Glaube* II (Tübingen, 1969), pp. 343–71.

M. Evang, *Rudolf Bultmann in seiner Frühzeit* (Tübingen, 1988).

C.F. Evans, 'Review of R. Bultmann's *The Gospel of John*' in *Scottish Journal of Theology* 26 (1973), pp. 341–9.

D. Fergusson, 'Meaning, truth and realism in Bultmann and Lindbeck', *Religious Studies* 26 (1990), pp. 183–98.

D. Ford (ed.), *Modern Theologians* I (Oxford, 1989).

D.B. Forrester, *Theology and Politics* (Oxford, 1988).

R.T. Fortna, *The Gospel of Signs* (Cambridge, 1970).

E. Frank, *Philosophical Understanding and Religious Truth* (New York, 1945).

H. Frei, *The Eclipse of Biblical Narrative* (New Haven, 1974).

E. Fuchs, *Studies of the Historical Jesus* (London, 1964).

Hermeneutik (Tübingen, 1970).

H.G. Gadamer, *Truth and Method* (London, 1975).

D. Georgi, 'Rudolf Bultmann's *Theology of the New Testament* revisited' in E.C. Hobbs (ed.), *Bultmann: Retrospect and Prospect* (Philadelphia, 1985).

F. Gogarten, 'Between the times' in J. Robinson (ed.), *The Beginnings of Dialectical Theology* (Richmond, 1968).

Demythologizing and History (London, 1955).

C. Guignon, *Heidegger and the Problem of Knowledge* (Indianapolis, 1983).

Van A. Harvey, *The Historian and the Believer* (London, 1967).

M. Heidegger, *Being and Time*, ed. J. Macquarrie and E. Robinson (Oxford, 1962).

R. Hepburn, 'Demythologizing and the problem of validity' in A. Flew and A. MacIntyre (eds), *New Essays in Philosophical Theology* (London, 1955).

A. Heron, *A Century of Protestant Theology* (London, 1980).

W. Herrmann, *Schriften zur Grundlegung der Theologie* II (Munich, 1967).

J. Hick, 'Jesus and the world religions' in *Myth of God Incarnate* (London, 1977), pp. 167–85.

H.A. Hodges, *Wilhelm Dilthey* (London, 1969).

E. Hobbs (ed.), *Bultmann: Retrospect and Prospect* (Philadelphia, 1985).

H. Hübner, *Politische Theologie* (Witten, 1973).

D. Hume, *An Enquiry Concerning Human Understanding*, ed. L.A. Selby-Bigge (Oxford, 1975).

G. Ittel, 'Der Einfluss der Philosophie M. Heideggers auf die Theologie R. Bultmanns' in *Kerygma und Dogma* (1956).

K. Jaspers, 'Myth and religion', K & M II, pp. 133–80.

B. Jaspert, 'Rudolf Bultmanns Wende von der liberalen Theologie zur dialektischen Theologie' in B. Jaspert (ed.), *Rudolf Bultmanns Werk und Wirkung* (Darmstadt, 1984).

R. Johnson, *The Origins of Demythologising* (Leiden, 1974).
(ed.), *Rudolf Bultmann—Interpreting Faith for the Modern Era* (London, 1987).

H. Jonas, 'Is faith still possible? Memories of Rudolf Bultmann and reflections on the philosophical aspects of his work', *Harvard Theological Review* 75 (1982), pp. 1–23.

G. Jones, *Bultmann: Towards a Critical Theology* (Oxford, 1991).

E. Jüngel, *Glauben und Verstehen—Zum Theologiebegriff Rudolf Bultmanns* (Heidelberg, 1985).

M. Kähler, *The So-Called Historical Jesus and the Historic Biblical Christ*, ed. C.F. Braaten (Philadelphia, 1964).

I. Kant, *Critique of Pure Reason*, ed. N. Kemp-Smith (London, 1929).

E. Käsemann, *Essays on New Testament Themes* (London, 1964).
New Testament Questions of Today (London, 1969).
The Testament of Jesus (London, 1968).
Perspectives on Paul (London, 1971).

C.W. Kegley (ed.), *The Theology of Rudolf Bultmann* (London, 1966).

F. Kerr, *Theology After Wittgenstein* (Oxford, 1987).

S. Kierkegaard, *Fear and Trembling* (Princeton, 1963).
Philosophical Fragments (Princeton, 1974).

M. King, *Heidegger's Philosophy: A Guide to His Basic Thought* (Oxford, 1964).

H. Koester, 'Early Christianity from the perspective of the history of religions: Rudolf Bultmann's contribution' in E.C. Hobbs (ed.), *Bultmann: Retrospect and Prospect* (Philadelphia, 1985), pp. 59–74.

G. Krause, 'Dietrich Bonhoeffer and Rudolf Bultmann' in J. Robinson (ed.), *The Future of Our Religious Past* (London, 1971), pp. 279–305.

G. Lessing, *Lessing's Theological Writings* ed. H. Chadwick (London, 1956).

G. Lindbeck, *The Nature of Doctrine* (London, 1984).

A. McGrath, *The Making of Modern German Christology* (Oxford, 1986).

J. P. Mackey, *Jesus: The Man and the Myth* (London, 1979).

E. V. McKnight, *What is Form Criticism?* (Philadelphia, 1969).

J. Macquarrie, *An Existentialist Theology* (London, 1955).

The Scope of Demythologizing (London, 1960).

'Philosophy and theology in Bultmann's thought' in C. W. Kegley (ed.), *The Theology of Rudolf Bultmann* (London, 1966), pp. 127–43.

Thinking About God (London, 1975).

A. Malet, *The Thought of Rudolf Bultmann* (Shannon, 1969).

I. H. Marshall, *New Testament Interpretation* (Exeter, 1977).

J. Metz, *Theology of the World* (New York, 1969).

J. Moltmann, *The Theology of Hope* (London, 1967).

The Crucified God (London, 1974).

The Church in the Power of the Spirit (London, 1977).

R. Morgan, *The Nature of New Testament Theology* (London, 1973).

'Rudolf Bultmann' in D. Ford (ed.), *Modern Theologians* (Oxford, 1989), pp. 109ff.

R. Morgan and J. Barton, *Biblical Interpretation* (Oxford, 1988).

J. C. O'Neill, 'Bultmann and Hegel', *Journal of Theological Studies* 21 (1970), pp. 387–400.

The Bible's Authority: A Portrait Gallery of Thinkers from Lessing to Bultmann (Edinburgh, 1991).

S. Ogden, *Christ Without Myth* (London, 1962).

The Point of Christology (London, 1982).

S. Ogden and Van A. Harvey, 'Wie neu ist die "Neue Frage nach dem historischen Jesus"?' in *Zeitschrift für Theologie und Kirche* 59 (1962), pp. 46–87.

H. Ott, *Geschichte und Heilsgeschichte in der Theologie Rudolf Bultmanns* (Tübingen, 1955).

'Objectification and existentialism', K & M II, pp. 306–35.

D. Pailin, *God and Processes of Reality* (London, 1989).

J. Painter, *Theology as Hermeneutics* (Sheffield, 1987).

R. Palmer, *Hermeneutics* (Evanston, 1969).

W. Pannenberg, 'On historical and theological hermeneutic' in *Basic Questions in Theology* I (London, 1970).

W. Placher, *Unapologetic Theology* (Louisville, 1989).

J. Richmond, *Ritschl: A Reappraisal* (London, 1978).

P. Ricoeur, 'Preface to Bultmann' in *The Conflict of Interpretations* (Evanston, 1974).

A. Ritschl, *The Christian Doctrine of Justification and Reconciliation*, ed. H.R. Mackintosh and A.B. Macaulay (Edinburgh, 1900).

J. Robinson (ed.), *The Beginnings of Dialectical Theology* (Richmond, 1968).

(ed.), *The Future of our Religious Past: Essays in Honour of Rudolf Bultmann* (London, 1971).

A New Quest of the Historical Jesus (London, 1959).

J.A.T. Robinson, *Honest to God* (London, 1963).

J.A.T. Robinson and D.L. Edwards, *The Honest to God Debate* (London, 1965).

C. Rowland and M. Corner, *Liberating Exegesis* (London, 1990).

E.P. Sanders, *Paul and Palestinian Judaism* (London, 1977).

E. Schillebeeckx, *Jesus: An Experiment in Christology* (London, 1979).

F. Schleiermacher, *The Christian Faith*, ed. H.R. Mackintosh and J.S. Stewart (Edinburgh, 1928).

Hermeneutics: The Handwritten Manuscripts, ed. H. Kimmerle (Missoula, MT, 1977).

W. Schmithals, *An Introduction to the Theology of Rudolf Bultmann* (London, 1968).

'Ein Brief Rudolf Bultmanns an Erich Foerster' in *Rudolf Bultmanns Werk und Wirkung* (Darmstadt, 1984), pp. 70–80.

Neues Testament und Gnosis (Darmstadt, 1988).

K. Scholder, *The Churches and the Third Reich* I–II (London, 1987–89).

E. Schürer, *History of the Jewish People* (5 vols; Edinburgh, 1885–91).

A. Schweitzer, *The Quest of the Historical Jesus* (London, 1911).

E. Schweizer, *Jesus* (London, 1971).

'Zur Interpretation des Kreuzes bei R. Bultmann' in *Aux Sources de la Tradition Chrétienne* (Neuchâtel, 1950), pp. 228–38.

D.M. Smith, *The Order and Composition of the Fourth Gospel: Bultmann's Literary Theory* (New Haven, 1965).

Johannine Christology (Columbia, 1984).

D. Sölle, *Political Theology* (Philadelphia, 1974).

G. Stanton, 'Form criticism' in M.D. Hooker and C. Hickling (eds), *What About the New Testament?* (London, 1975).

The Gospels and Jesus (Oxford, 1989).

J. Stevenson (ed.), *A New Eusebius* (London, 1983).

P. Stuhlmacher, *Jesus von Nazareth—Christus des Glaubens* (Stuttgart, 1988).

S. Travis, 'Form criticism' in I. H. Marshall (ed.), *New Testament Interpretation* (Exeter, 1977), pp. 153-64.

E. Troeltsch, *Writings on Theology and Religion*, ed. R. Morgan and M. Pye (London, 1977).

F. Watson, *Paul, Judaism and Gentiles* (Cambridge, 1986).

C. Welch, *Protestant Thought in the Nineteenth Century* I-II (New Haven, 1972-85).

S. Westerholm, *Israel's Law and the Church's Faith* (Grand Rapids, 1988).

U. Wilckens, 'Christologie und Anthropologie im Zusammenhang der paulinischen Rechtfertigungslehre', *Zeitschrift für die neutestamentliche Wissenschaft* 67 (1976), pp. 64-82.

R. McL. Wilson, *Gnosis and the New Testament* (Oxford, 1968).

L. Wittgenstein, *Philosophical Investigations* (Oxford, 1958).

T. Witvliet, *A Place in the Sun* (London, 1985).

ABBREVIATIONS OF MAJOR WORKS OF BULTMANN

EF	*Existence and Faith*
EPT	*Essays Philosophical and Theological*
Ex	*Exegetica*
FU	*Faith and Understanding*
GJ	*The Gospel of John*
GV	*Glauben und Verstehen* (4 vols)
HST	*History of the Synoptic Tradition*
JCM	*Jesus Christ and Mythology*
Jesus	*Jesus and the Word*
K & M	*Kerygma and Myth* (2 vols) ed. Bartsch
KuM	*Kergyma und Mythos* (6 vols) ed. Bartsch
Letters	*Karl Barth–Rudolf Bultmann: Letters 1922–66*
NTM	*New Testament and Mythology and Other Basic Writings*
PCCS	*Primitive Christianity in its Contemporary Setting*
TE	*Theologische Enzyklopädie*
TNT	*Theology of the New Testament* (2 vols)

Full details of these and other works of Bultmann are cited in the bibliography.

1

Introduction

Rudolf Karl Bultmann was born on 30 July 1884 in Wiefelstede, near Oldenburg, in the north of Germany. He was the son of a Lutheran pastor, Arthur Bultmann, and his wife, Helene.[1] Rudolf was educated at the local gymnasium in Oldenburg, 1895–1903, and from there he proceeded to university as a student of theology. His theological education followed the German pattern of studying in several institutions, and in doing so he gained a thorough grounding in the various theological disciplines, particularly New Testament studies and systematic theology. Three semesters were spent in Tübingen, two in Berlin and a further two in Marburg. His teachers included many of the leading scholars of the day: Karl Müller and Theodor Haering in Tübingen; Adolf Harnack, Hermann Gunkel and Julius Kaftan in Berlin; Johannes Weiss and Wilhelm Herrmann in Marburg.

Bultmann's most distinguished teachers belonged to the liberal school of theology and biblical criticism which had emanated from Göttingen in the late nineteenth century. The focus of liberal theology was the journal *Die Christliche Welt*. Bultmann belonged to the journal's society, 'Freunde der Christlichen Welt', and during his time in Marburg he came into close contact with the editor, Martin Rade. In subsequent years, he became a regular contributor to the journal. Liberal theology formed the background to Bultmann's own thought which developed in a sustained and critical dialogue with his teachers. Although inspired by them with a passion for his subject, he never ceased to criticize and to revise their presuppositions when he believed it necessary.[2]

1

Bultmann's primary expertise was as a New Testament scholar, trained in the history of religions school. In 1910 he completed his qualifying dissertation, begun under Johannes Weiss, and entitled 'Die Stil der paulinischen Predigt und die kynisch–stoische Diatribe'.[3] Two years later, he qualified as a lecturer in New Testament studies with the completion of his Habilitationsschrift, 'Die Exegese des Theodor von Mopsuestia'.[4]

His academic career progressed in a manner typical of the German university system. He taught as a junior lecturer in Marburg from 1912 to 1916, as an associate professor in Breslau from 1916 to 1920, and as a professor in Giessen 1920 to 1921, before returning to Marburg in 1921. In 1917, while in Breslau, he married Helene Feldman (1892–1973) from Essen. They had a family of three daughters. Marburg was Bultmann's intellectual home from his student days onwards and he continued to live there after his retirement in 1951. A street was named after him in 1984 on the centenary of his birth.[5]

Bultmann's biblical and theological scholarship were carried out in the heart of Europe during one of the most turbulent periods of its history. He lived in Germany during two world wars, the Third Reich, the Holocaust, and the partition of East and West Germany. While his writings tend not to reveal the direct impact of these events, they were nevertheless keenly felt. Bultmann lost one of his brothers in the First World War and the other in a concentration camp in 1942. He himself did not see active wartime service because of a congenital hip defect, but during the 1930s he was involved as a member of the Confessing Church in the German Church struggle. It was then that he broke his customary political silence to speak against the persecution of Jews. His opposition to the Nazi regime probably cemented his friendship with Karl Barth but led to a cooling of relations with Martin Heidegger.[6] We shall examine Bultmann's relationship to National Socialism more closely in Chapter 3.

Following his retirement, he travelled in the United States in 1951 and delivered the Schaffer Lectures at Yale Divinity School. In 1955, he journeyed to Britain to deliver the Gifford Lectures at Edinburgh University.[7] Throughout his later years, he continued to engage in lively dialogue and correspondence with former students and critics. He died on 30 July 1976, shortly before his 92nd birthday.

Bultmann's extensive correspondence is mostly held in the library of Tübingen University. While little has yet been published, it reveals his lifelong commitment to the Church and his willingness to engage in dialogue with people from a wide variety of backgrounds.[8] Bultmann appears to have been an earnest, serious-minded scholar with a passion for intellectual honesty, and a teacher who won the admiration and gratitude of generations of students. Unfortunately no biography has yet been written of him, but perhaps these moving words of his Jewish student, Hans Jonas, give us some insight into the man.

> Bultmann was the only one of my academic teachers to whom I paid a farewell visit before my emigration. It was in the summer of 1933, here in Marburg. We sat around the dinner table with his lovely, so richly emotional wife and the three schoolgirl daughters, and I related what I had just read in the newspaper, but he not yet, namely, that the German Association of the Blind had expelled its Jewish members. My horror carried me into eloquence: In the face of eternal night (so I exclaimed), the most unifying tie there can be among suffering men, this betrayal of the solidarity of a common fate—and I stopped, for my eye fell on Bultmann and I saw that a deathly pallor had spread over his face, and in his eyes was such agony that the words died in my mouth. In that moment I knew that in matters of elementary humanity one could simply rely on Bultmann, that words, explanations, arguments, most of all rhetoric, were out of place here, that no insanity of the time could dim the steadiness of his inner light. He himself had not said a word. Ever since, this episode has belonged to the image of the inwardly moved but outwardly so unemotional man.[9]

Bultmann's work was a towering achievement. He was amongst the leaders of many of the dominant trends in twentieth-century theology; he wrote as a form critic, a dialectical theologian, an existentialist, a Lutheran, and the original exponent of the demythologizing of the New Testament—a programme that gained him fame and notoriety throughout the Western Churches. His work embodies a fascinating commitment to the ancient Christian tradition and to the ineluctable challenges it faces in the modern world. In our study of his thought we shall be attempting to see how his various writings form a complex unity. The different themes that we shall encounter can be read as essentially harmonious. We shall begin by examining the historical background to his theology and then we shall sketch its overall shape. The later chapters will deal

3

with more specific aspects of his writings, and, in conclusion, we shall consider the central criticisms of his work.

Notes

1 Published sources on Bultmann's life include his own 'Autobiographical reflections' in EF, pp.335–41 and the extended version in C.W. Kegley (ed), *Theology of Rudolf Bultmann* (London, 1966), pp. xix–xxv; *Karl Barth–Rudolf Bultmann: Letters, 1922–66*, ed. B. Jaspert (Edinburgh, 1982); Antje Bultmann Lemke, 'Der unveröffentlichte Nachlass von Rudolf Bultmann' in Bernd Jaspert (ed.), *Rudolf Bultmanns Werk und Wirkung* (Darmstadt, 1984), pp. 194–207, and 'Bultmann's papers' in E.C. Hobbs (ed.), *Bultmann: Retrospect and Prospect* (Philadelphia, 1985), pp. 3–12; Walter Schmithals, *An Introduction to the Theology of Rudolf Bultmann* (London, 1968), ch. 1; Martin Evang, *Rudolf Bultmann in seiner Frühzeit* (Tübingen, 1988).

2 The evolution of Bultmann's theology from his student days is meticulously analysed by Martin Evang, op. cit. A helpful sketch of his relationship to the theological and historical work of his teachers can be found in Robert Morgan, 'Rudolf Bultmann' in D. Ford (ed.), *Modern Theologians* (Oxford, 1989), pp. 109ff. In his recent study, John O'Neill provides an excellent overview of Bultmann's work set in the context of his life and times: *The Bible's Authority: A Portrait Gallery of Thinkers from Lessing to Bultmann* (Edinburgh, 1991), pp. 284–309.

3 *Der Stil der paulinischen Predigt und die kynisch-stoische Diatribe* (Göttingen, 1984). This early dissertation, comparing the style of the Pauline sermon with the Cynic–Stoical diatribe, reflects Bultmann's grounding in the history of religions school.

4 *Die Exegese des Theodor von Mopsuestia* (Stuttgart, 1984).

5 For Bultmann's own reflections on his time at Marburg University see *Letters*, pp. 161–2.

6 Cf. W. Schmithals, op. cit.

7 For Bultmann's US itinerary and his subsequent report of the lecture tour to the Marburg theology faculty see *Letters*, pp. 148–50. His Schaffer Lectures were published as *Jesus Christ and Mythology* (New York, 1958), his Gifford Lectures in Britain as *History and Eschatology* (Edinburgh, 1957) and in the USA as *The Presence of Eternity* (New York, 1957).

8 Antje Bultmann Lemke, op. cit.

9 'Is faith still possible? Memories of Rudolf Bultmann and reflections on the philosophical aspects of his work', *Harvard Theological Review*, 75 (1982), pp. 2–3.

2

The legacy of liberalism

The student of Bultmann's theology is often puzzled by its richness and complexity. At times, Bultmann speaks as a Lutheran preacher when he claims that the word of God bears down upon us in our fallen state, so that we may not question it but only hear it and receive it. At other times, he seems to speak as a radical critic of the New Testament when he asserts that we know little or nothing of Jesus' self-consciousness, and that vast areas of the New Testament are shot through with the mythological categories of the writers. At other times still, Bultmann speaks as an existentialist philosopher insisting that human existence is marked by anxiety and the search for false securities, and that freedom is realized only in the honest recognition of this anxiety, accompanied by the commitment to live authentically. We find in these three different strands of his thought a complexity which can confuse and frustrate the reader. Nevertheless, we can see clearly the extent to which these strands are interwoven when we have contextualized his thought. In large measure, the positions Bultmann adopts are in response to problems and insights he perceived in the theology of the nineteenth and early twentieth centuries. It is to this historical context that we must first turn in order to appreciate his thought.[1]

The Enlightenment critique of religion

The Enlightenment was a widespread cultural movement in eighteenth-century Europe which challenged the authority of the Bible, the Church and Christian theology. Its guiding principle was a confident belief in the power of human reason to ascertain truth. It was within the capacity of each rational being to consider the evidence, to assess the arguments, and to distinguish truth from error. This access to knowledge challenged the nature of authority. Authority no longer resided in either the Bible or the Church, but in the reason and conscience of the individual enquirer. This created problems for theologians in three areas.

(1) *The Bible*. The remarkable advances in science made by men like Copernicus, Galileo and Newton came into conflict with the popular notion that the Bible was an infallible source of scientific, moral and theological truth. If Copernicus was right, then the earth did not stand motionless at the centre of the solar system, and the sun could not have stood still in the sky while Joshua's army took vengeance on their enemies. Doubts began to emerge about the literal truth of the six days of creation recorded in the opening chapter of Genesis, while the gradual success of the experimental method of reason employed by Newton suggested that the Bible was no longer necessary as a divinely bestowed scientific textbook. The natural sciences could, on occasion, contradict the Bible with the latter generally being the loser.

In addition to difficulties created by the natural sciences, the development of the methods of historical criticism posed further problems for the sacred Scriptures of Christendom. As texts came under the scrutiny of literary analysis and historical comparison, further awkward questions emerged. Did Moses write the Pentateuch? Were there not internal contradictions within some of the books themselves? Were the gospels written by eye-witnesses of the events depicted? Did they provide historically reliable accounts of what Jesus had actually said and done? For defenders of the faith these questions were painful yet unavoidable. Indeed, as we shall shortly see, the theologians of the nineteenth century were preoccupied by the theological problems raised by biblical criticism, and Bultmann, dissatisfied with many of their proposals, found himself responding in a novel way to the same set of problems.

(2) *Miracles*. For centuries, theologians had been in the habit of appealing to miracles as signs and confirmations of the biblical message. The parting of the Red Sea confirmed that God was with the Israelites in their escape from Egyptian bondage. The miracles performed by Jesus confirmed his divinity. His resurrection from the grave was the final seal on his victory over sin, death and the

legions of hell. The mighty works performed by the apostles testified to the power of the Holy Spirit. Yet the rise of both scientific and historical study called this style of apologetic argument into question. This provided a philosopher like David Hume with a two-pronged fork with which to attack his religious opponents.

According to Hume, reports of miracles abounded principally among primitive and superstitious peoples.[2] Moreover, the regularity in the laws of nature perceived by the experimental sciences told decisively against a belief in the miraculous. It is always more reasonable, Hume argued, to believe that a scientific explanation is simply concealed from us than that a miracle has taken place. In the case of the resurrection, it is more probable that the witnesses were erroneous than that the regularity of natural law was breached. This impression seems to be confirmed by the study of human nature and history.

The scientific view of the world which emerges from the Enlightenment tends to be one in which every event is governed rigidly by the laws of nature. The material universe is a closed causal continuum immune from the occasional acts of supernatural agencies. The natural world which the scientist surveys is not one in which God is seen to intervene. The confident removal of God from the scientific view of the universe was expressed in Laplace's celebrated claim that he had 'no need of that hypothesis'. In much of the theology of the nineteenth century, this view is tacitly accepted and we find it being endorsed in Bultmann's own theology. God cannot be inferred from miraculous signs which breach the intrinsic regularity of nature. The divine presence is not apparent in this way.

(3) *The dismantling of the proofs for God's existence.* A further significant feature of Enlightenment thought was the philosophical onslaught upon the traditional arguments for the existence of God. These arguments were first promulgated by the philosophers of ancient Greece and then taken up by Christian thinkers. They were affirmed throughout the Middle Ages and were defended by Descartes in the seventeenth century. The Enlightenment, however, levelled a barrage of criticism against these proofs, principally through the work of David Hume and Immanuel Kant.

The three traditional proofs of God's existence were the ontological, the cosmological and the design arguments. The ontological proof sought to establish the existence of God upon the peculiar type of necessity attending God's mode of being. This argument was criticized as a sophisticated conjuring trick in which the existence of

God was produced from the very idea of God. According to Kant, this was a misuse of the concept of existence; from the mere idea of an entity we can never deduce its existence. The cosmological proof sought to demonstrate God's existence as a necessary explanation for the contingent universe. Since nothing can come out of nothing, something must explain the existence of the world. The problem with this, however, was in showing the incoherence of conceiving of the universe as an unexplained brute fact. Perhaps, speculated Hume, the universe had always existed or had merely sprung into being by chance. The design argument appealed to the order and harmony of the world as conclusive evidence of a Creator God. Yet, here again, it was claimed that the design may simply have been accidental or have arisen in other ways.[3]

Whether or not these criticisms were justified, it is clear that they had a profound effect upon subsequent theology. It was no longer assumed that philosophy could undergird by metaphysical argument the claims of religion. Rational demonstration could not now be given to theological conclusions. As a consequence of this, theologians looked to other sources, principally moral and religious experience, in order to construct their systems. Bultmann's theology wholeheartedly embraces this turn towards personal experience and encounter, although it is construed in a manner that reflects his dissatisfaction with nineteenth-century theology. For Bultmann, philosophical proof is not something that the theologian should aspire to. It represents an attempt to locate God where God cannot be discerned.

Liberal theology

The term 'liberal theology' is an elusive one. It is sometimes used, loosely and pejoratively, to refer to any theology that is suspiciously unorthodox. More properly, it may be used to refer to a broad stream of theology from Schleiermacher onwards which responds to the Enlightenment challenge by construing religious or moral experience as the primary locus for our knowledge of God. A third and more technical use of the term 'liberal theology' is its application to the loosely-defined school of Albrecht Ritschl which dominated European theology around the period 1875 to 1920. It is in this more technical sense that we shall use the term. But, first, it is necessary to mention the significance of Schleiermacher.

Friedrich Schleiermacher (1768–1834)

Schleiermacher has been described as 'the father of modern theology'. In his work we see a positive Christian response both to the scepticism of the Enlightenment and to the aridity of orthodox theological systems. While Kant had argued that religion still had a place as an aid to morality, Schleiermacher insisted upon the uniqueness and peculiarity of the religious impulse. The roots of religion are to be found neither in knowing (the mind), nor in doing (the moral will), but in the realm of feeling.

The uniqueness of the religious impulse was located in 'the consciousness of being absolutely dependent, or which is the same thing, of being in relation with God'.[4] This consciousness of absolute dependence constitutes the religious awareness of each individual, and undergirds all thought and action. Our descriptions of God are essentially ways of articulating this original experience. For the Christian, all talk of God is related to the way in which our religious experience is determined by our awareness of Jesus Christ. Through membership of the Christian community, we enter into fellowship with its founder, and, in particular, with the power of his God-consciousness. Schleiermacher argued that the gospels present us with a human being in whom the consciousness of God is complete and all-controlling. In others it is broken and suppressed by lower impulses, but in Christ the consciousness of God is sovereign and perfect. The Church as the community which lives in communion with Christ is infected and transformed by the power of his God-consciousness. Accordingly, the doctrines of the Christian faith are understood as the expressions of this distinctive experience of God. 'Christian doctrines are accounts of the Christian religious affections set forth in speech.'[5]

The importance of Schleiermacher's work was that it set Christian theology on a new basis. It was no longer established upon a philosophical system or upon a theory about the revealed propositions of Scripture. Its basis lay within the unique religious experience of the individual. It was grounded upon the living testimony of the individual in the particular circumstances of his or her life. This dual emphasis upon the particular situation of the individual and the distinctiveness of religious experience is a hallmark of much nineteenth-century theology, and is carried over into the theology of Bultmann.

Albrecht Ritschl (1822–89)

Much of Ritschl's early work was as an historical critic of the New Testament but his main contribution lay in the theology he developed during his time in Göttingen after 1864. Ritschl was in agreement with Schleiermacher's method of beginning with the experience of the individual believer, yet he considered that this must be approached through the historical study of the earliest Christian witnesses, rather than through the inner feelings of the religious subject. According to Ritschl, it is upon the value judgements of individuals as they are confronted by the witness of the gospels that faith is grounded. This primary focus upon Christ and the community he established enables Ritschl to display the moral and communal dimension of the Christian religion. In this respect, his work is closer to Kant than to Schleiermacher.

The two key themes that Ritschl discerned in the gospels were Jesus' relationship to God and the message of the kingdom which arose thereby. These two themes are inseparably linked in the life of Jesus, and in the life of the Christian. Through his oneness with God, Jesus was able to overcome the contradictions of human nature, thus inaugurating in his dealings with others the moral kingdom. Jesus' union with God, together with the community he created, are what set Christianity apart from every other religion. Insofar as he is the bearer of the presence of God and his kingdom, Jesus has the *value* of God for us. The idea of the incarnation is thus a value judgement of faith.

> Thus what in the historically complete figure of Christ we recognize to be the real worth of his existence, gains for ourselves, through the uniqueness of the phenomenon and its normative bearing upon our religious ethical destiny, the worth of an abiding rule, since we at the same time discover that only through the impulse and direction we receive from him, is it possible for us to enter into his relation to God and to the world.[6]

In the study of the gospels the individual enquirer is faced with these phenomena. The truths of the Christian faith are functions of the practical value judgements made by the Christian. In this respect, faith belongs to the concrete and particular setting of individual life. As in Schleiermacher, it is not to be seen as the acknowledgement of a philosophical theory or the acceptance of dogmatic propositions. Faith only arises as the individual makes value judgements of the New Testament witness. 'Whosoever willeth to do the will of God, will know that the doctrine of Christ is true.'[7]

Ritschl's liberal theology is distinguished by a number of characteristics. Firstly, it attaches primary significance to the moral and religious experience of the individual enquirer. Faith is grounded upon this, rather than upon philosophy or propositional orthodoxy. Secondly, the historical study of the gospels emerges as a crucial task for the theologian. Ritschl's theology depends upon a particular reading of the gospels regarding the religious life and teaching of Jesus. Indeed, it depends upon the historical validity of the claim that in the life and teaching of Jesus we encounter a faith that stands apart from any other religious personality. Thirdly, Ritschl's theology assumes that these truths presented in the New Testament can be recognized and endorsed by the historical enquirer making value judgements.

One of the central difficulties that arose for liberal theology was the way in which historical study came to cast doubt on the second of these claims. This, together with theological difficulties surrounding the third claim, led Bultmann beyond liberal theology. But, to see this more clearly, it is necessary to look briefly at the theology of Herrmann, Bultmann's teacher and colleague in Marburg.

Wilhelm Herrmann (1846–1922)
Herrmann was one of the leading exponents of liberal theology at the turn of the century. As the theological teacher of both Barth and Bultmann, his influence upon the subsequent development of twentieth-century theology is considerable. Herrmann re-emphasized the claim of Ritschl that the world of religion was unique and could not be assimilated to either science or philosophy. He insisted that the task of science and philosophy is to understand and explain the features of the public, empirical world. By contrast, religion is concerned with the practical transformation of the inner life. Faith arises not through scientific or metaphysical explanation, but only through the religious experience of personal life. Theology is based solely upon this and does not require to be supported by philosophy.

> Knowledge of God . . . is not generally valid or provable knowledge, but is the defenceless expression of individual experience.[8]

For the Christian, faith is formed through the power of the personality of Jesus working upon one's inner life. Through the medium of the gospels, the influence of Jesus' religious consciousness impresses itself upon us. This power of Jesus is the vital principle of the believer's faith. As in Ritschl, it has a significant moral

11

dimension. In submitting to the love of God in Christ we are enabled to live for others under the fatherly rule of God. This is the message of the kingdom, as preached by Jesus.

The notion of faith as 'trust' is central to Herrmann's thought. Faith is not to be viewed as the assent of the mind to dogmatic propositions or even to the words of Scripture. It is not to be construed as the intellectual acceptance of a Christian world-view as if theology were a grand cosmological hypothesis. Faith is to be understood as personal trust in the power of Jesus. Consequently, the language of theology must be viewed only as the expression of such individual, personal experience. In this respect, we know of God only as God's power impinges upon our experience. This account of faith has strong Lutheran overtones. Melanchthon, Luther's disciple and colleague, claimed that to know Christ is to know his benefits, as opposed to understanding a dogmatic theory about the union of two natures in his person. This is echoed by Herrmann. Faith involves a practical, personal knowledge of Christ rather than the understanding of a theory. Any attempt to prove the validity of faith by either philosophy or science can only resemble a desire to be justified by works rather than by faith alone. Herrmann regards this as a legitimate extension of the doctrine of justification into the realm of epistemology. Here he is closely followed by Bultmann, and, in this respect, his theology is perhaps the most important single influence upon Bultmann.[9]

Yet, while Herrmann's epistemology is to a large extent carried over into Bultmann's theology, the historical problems that Herrmann encountered lead to some striking differences in Bultmann. In this context we should consider the work of Martin Kähler (1835–1912) and Ernst Troeltsch (1865–1923). In the second edition of *The So-Called Historical Jesus and the Historic, Biblical Christ* (1896), Kähler levelled some powerful criticisms against the theology of Herrmann.[10] His central charge was that the historical sources do not yield the kind of information about Jesus that Herrmann's theology requires. The earliest Christians, Kähler argued, were not so much interested in biographical details about the personality of Jesus as in proclaiming the message of his death and resurrection. Paul, for instance, tells us very little about the life of Jesus, while the gospels have scant interest in the major portion of his life. Indeed, with the exception of the incident in the Temple when he was twelve years old, the gospels are silent on the life of Jesus in the period between his birth and the commencement of his ministry. The New Testament is naturally preoccupied with the

Christ who is proclaimed in the preaching of the earliest Christians. It witnesses to his death and resurrection, rather than probes into his religious self-consciousness. The inner life of Jesus, so central to Herrmann's Christology, is not a dominant theme of the New Testament. Thus our sources do not supply us with the kind of information that Herrmann is looking for.

Troeltsch was one of the leading representatives of the 'history of religions school' (*Religionsgeschichtliche Schule*). This school of thought attempted to understand the origins of the Christian religion within the context of first-century culture. Troeltsch was one of the more philosophical thinkers of the school and, while an admirer of Herrmann's theology, he raised some important questions of it. In particular, his sensitivity to the manner in which all ethical and religious ideas belonged to a particular historical setting led him to ask whether Herrmann's own religious and ethical sensibilities might themselves reflect rather closely late nineteenth-century German culture. Moreover, the way in which all religion is embedded in a particular cultural setting raised the further question of whether it was ever proper to assign an absolute validity to the religion of the historical Jesus.

> This entanglement of Christianity in the wider context of the history of religions with all its analogies and real connexions, and in the currents of ordinary practical and intellectual life, places it completely in the stream of the historical process. The question then arises how far its religious idea and power is in any respect ultimate, perfect and absolute. The concepts of revelation and redemption asserted by the older liberalism and by Schleiermacher, though in the form of absolute religion breaking through rather than as a miracle opposed to all the rest of history, are thus threatened by being drawn into the fluctuations of revelation in ordinary spiritual life. It becomes a question how far Christianity as such is a definitive religious phenomenon which completes everything. It therefore becomes a question too how far it is to be seen as revelation and redemption in the absolute sense.[11]

Troeltsch argued that the study of all religious history must be informed by the three principles of criticism, analogy and correlation. *Criticism* requires that no evidence is ever immune from being challenged. In principle, the historian must always be willing to revise conclusions. The principle of *analogy* presupposes that every event under investigation is similar in kind to events we have experienced ourselves. Without this presupposition there can be no historical understanding. The principle of *correlation* assumes that events are inter-connected in a vast network of relations. Thus, every event has a context, and only in relation to that context does the event have meaning. The cumulative effect of Troeltsch's three principles is that it becomes impossible for the historian to identify any one expression of religion as absolute for all others. This represented an enormous stumbling block for liberal theology which had assumed that the historical study of the gospels could lead to the recognition of the one true religion, namely the religion of Jesus. The Christian theologian either has to lapse into a form of relativism, or else find some other route by which to proclaim the absoluteness of Christianity. Bultmann, as we shall see, opts for the latter alternative with his insistence upon the word of God as the recurring possibility of each moment of human existence. Revelation is not tied to the past and discerned through historical investigation; it is a dynamic encounter in the existential present.

The quest of the historical Jesus

These criticisms levelled against Herrmann indicate the impact of historical scholarship upon the course of nineteenth-century theology. This is nowhere more apparent than in the quest for the historical Jesus. Before examining some of the details of the quest, it is worth pausing to note some of the philosophical issues that informed the application of historical criticism to the Bible.

The most immediate concern regarding the historical investigation of New Testament texts was over the question whether the historian's excavation of the tradition would reveal a picture of Jesus which corresponded with the accounts of the gospels. The thought that the historical Jesus might turn out to be radically different from the traditional picture of faith was both exciting and disconcerting. Yet in addition to this, there were more subtle questions concerning the relation of faith to history, posed by the philosopher Gotthold Lessing (1729–81). In one famous phrase, he spoke of the 'ugly, broad ditch of history'[12] by which our access to the past was only indirect and through evidence that was at best probable. A further difficulty concerned the contingent nature of all historical events. Experience teaches us that historical events happen not by necessity but by accident. For example, if circumstances had been different William might not have won the Battle of

Hastings in 1066, nor Robert Bruce the Battle of Bannockburn in 1314. In the light of this, it is hard to understand how timeless and necessary truths regarding the being of God could be founded upon the un-necessary events of history. Thus, according to Lessing, 'accidental truths of history can never become the proof of necessary truths of reason'.[13]

The history of the quest for the historical Jesus is best seen from the perspective of Albert Schweitzer's classic study *The Quest of the Historical Jesus* (1906), which surveyed a series of attempts to discern the life of Jesus from a critical study of the New Testament, beginning with Reimarus in the 1770s and ending with Wilhelm Wrede in 1901. Schweitzer describes movingly how painful and bitter were many of the disputes involved in the critical study of the gospels.

> We can at the present day, scarcely imagine the long agony in which the historical view of the life of Jesus came to birth.[14]

In the end, however, although seeing the quest as one of the outstanding achievements of German culture, Schweitzer's conclusions were disappointingly negative. He summarized the quest by identifying three areas of concern.

(1) *The question of miracles.* For many years, a battle had raged between those who favoured a literal, supernatural explanation of the miracles and those who favoured a rationalist explanation. Heinrich Paulus, a rationalist scholar, had sought to 'explain away' the miracles, e.g. by providing a psychosomatic account of the healings performed by Jesus; by treating the walking on the water as an optical illusion in the early morning mist; and by construing the feeding of the five thousand as a sharing of previously concealed packed lunches. However, the dispute between rationalists and supernaturalists was overtaken by events following the publication of David Friedrich Strauss's *The Life of Jesus* (1835). Strauss argued that the miracles were to be seen as 'myths': stories set in historical form but expressing a religious idea. The gospels, he argued, had been written in such a way as to depict the belief that Jesus was divine. The healing stories had been expanded, the nature miracles had been invented, and the accounts of the transfiguration and the resurrection had been created to express a belief in Jesus' divinity.[15]

As a result of this reductionist treatment of the miracles, the importance of Jesus' life was subsequently believed to reside, not in the miraculous deeds of his divine nature, but rather in his religious personality, his ethical teaching and the changes he wrought in other people. Schweitzer described this as the 'psychologizing' approach to the historical Jesus. One of the most popular of the lives of Jesus which appeared was that of the Frenchman Ernest Renan. His *Life of Jesus* (1863) depicted Jesus as a romantic, poetic carpenter who uttered the most sublime teaching and was loved by a simple yet fair band of followers. In the face of opposition, he had to strengthen his cause by performing miracles, and he prepared his followers to become a church through instituting the sacrament of his body and blood. In the end, he surrendered himself to death but his religion renews itself in the lives of his followers. Renan's historical study thus produced a striking portrait of Jesus which differed from the traditional images of Christian piety. Its defect, however, was that it was too redolent of the spirit of the age in which it was written. Schweitzer complained that Renan had perfumed the world of the New Testament with sentimentality in order to feel at home in it.[16]

(2) *The four gospels.* The second area of controversy that Schweitzer observed concerned the relationship between the four gospels. From the time of F.C. Baur and the Tübingen school onwards, it had been recognized that the fourth gospel stood apart from the other three. Strauss, for instance, argued that the presentation of the fourth gospel was dominated not by a desire to reflect eye-witness accounts of Jesus' life but by a theory regarding the theological significance of that life. It is the theological purpose of the writer which selects, groups and even creates the subject-matter of the gospel. The long discourses from the mouth of Jesus reflect the theological message of the writer, rather than record what the historical Jesus had actually said. The content of these discourses, especially the 'I am' sayings, contrasts sharply with the message of the kingdom often set in parabolic form in the other three gospels. After Strauss, attention was given to the relationship between the first three gospels. C.H. Weisse presented a series of arguments for Marcan priority which are still widely accepted. Mark, he claimed, was the earliest of the three synoptic gospels and was used as a source by both Matthew and Luke.[17]

It was believed that the synoptic tradition was grounded upon two main sources: Mark and Q (a body of sayings which lay behind much of the material common only to Matthew and Luke). Mark, it was thought, provides us with a reliable account of the life of Jesus which can function as the historical bedrock for theological construction. The Christology of the liberal school hinged upon the credibility of something like this hypothesis. Yet this apparently unassailable position was eventually called into question by Wilhelm Wrede's *The Messianic Secret in the Gospels* (1901).

Wrede argued that Jesus had not regarded himself as the apocalyptic Son of Man (the recurrent title used by Jesus of himself in Mark) who would return to judge the earth and be exalted as Lord over all. This was a later belief of the early Church attributed retrospectively to Jesus. In order to explain why this was not widely known in Jesus' own lifetime they invented the motif of Jesus' messianic secrecy. His true identity was concealed to all but his disciples, and the entire gospel was written up to support this claim. Thus, according to Wrede, the narrative of Mark, no less than that of John, is controlled by the apologetic and theological purposes of the writer. Jesus, it seemed, was becoming ever more elusive, and the historical hypothesis required for the pursuit of liberal theology was suddenly crumbling. Schweitzer could write in 1906:

> Modern historical theology is no doubt still far from recognising this. It is warned that the dyke is letting in water and sends a couple of masons to repair the leak; as if the leak did not mean that the whole masonry is undermined, and must be rebuilt from the foundation.[18]

(3) *Eschatology.* Schweitzer's third focus of interest concerned the eschatology of Jesus and the New Testament. While the presence of eschatology had been noted since the time of Reimarus's *Fragment*, it was brought into the centre of the debate by the publication of Johannes Weiss's 'The Preaching of Jesus Concerning the Kingdom of God' (1892). Weiss argued that what Jesus meant by 'the kingdom of God' could only be understood within the setting of Jewish apocalyptic–eschatological thought. The end of the world was nigh, the judgement of God was imminent; and the kingdom would soon arrive through a divine interruption of history. Everything Jesus taught concerning the kingdom had to be seen in the light of this apocalyptic expectation. The Sermon on the Mount, for example, instructed people in how to prepare for the coming crisis. It was not presented as a universally valid moral code for successive generations, but in anticipation of the impending eschaton.[19]

The conclusions of Weiss's work were deeply disconcerting for liberal theology. (Weiss was the son-in-law of Albrecht Ritschl.) The universal moral community established by Jesus for all time was now called into question. The historical sources did not seem to provide the necessary warrants for the conclusions of liberal theology. The message of Jesus looked less like the moral code of the nineteenth-century European intellectual, and more like the claims of an ancient prophet belonging to a strange and alien culture.

Wrede, with his work on the history of the Christian tradition, and Weiss, with his work on the history of religions, had together pulled the rug from under the feet of liberal theology. The historical claims implicit in the theology of Ritschl, Herrmann and Harnack could not be supported by the New Testament scholars. Thus, the very historical study upon which Ritschl had claimed to base his theology led, in the event, to its demise. It is imperative to perceive Bultmann as a thinker in this historical tradition. As we have seen, he trained as a New Testament scholar rather than a systematic theologian, and it was through historical study that he came to appreciate the theological shortcomings of liberalism. His own theology emerges out of the difficulties that he perceived in his liberal ancestry, and it is grounded in his passionate commitment to traditio-historical criticism of the Bible. The theological proposals of liberalism may have been found wanting, yet the task of historical criticism had to be pursued with all the vigour and skill that the scholar could muster.

> Liberal theology owed its distinctive character chiefly to the primacy of *historical interest* and in that field it made its greatest contributions . . . We who have come from a background of liberal theology could never have become theologians nor remained such had we not encountered in that liberal theology the earnest search for radical truth. . . . Here, we felt, was the atmosphere of truth in which alone we could breathe.[20]

As a historian, Bultmann thus stood firmly in the tradition of liberal theology emerging from Göttingen. His *History of the Synoptic Tradition* (1921) was one of the great pioneer works of the new 'form criticism', and appeared before he came under the influence of dialectical theology. Alongside the works of Karl Ludwig Schmidt and Martin Dibelius, this was one of the most significant essays in shaping historical study of the gospels through the methods of form criticism, and it cannot be understood without reference to the prior work of Wrede, Weiss, Bousset and others.

Form criticism, a method originally worked out in relation to the

Old Testament, was grounded in the conviction that the gospels were composed of a collection of individual units which had originally been part of an older oral tradition. These units belonged to a particular *Sitz im Leben* (setting in life) of the early Christian communities and were shaped (formed) according to their needs and life-style. The task of the form critic was to analyse and classify the individual units in the light of their original setting in the life of the community. Once this setting had been established, it then became possible to theorize about the ways in which the individual units had been gathered, edited or even created by the community. To a large extent, the results of Bultmann's form criticism confirmed Wrede's scepticism regarding the historical Jesus. The primary explanation of the synoptic material referred to the situation of the early Church, rather than to the circumstances of the life of Jesus. We shall examine Bultmann's form criticism in greater detail in Chapter 5.

Dialectical theology

The term 'dialectical theology' refers to a movement that began around 1920 and which protested against the prevailing liberal theology. In addition to the intellectual forces outlined above, it was profoundly influenced by the horrors of the First World War (1914–18), which seemed to expose the optimism of the nineteenth century as naive and foolish. The leading exponents of dialectical theology were Karl Barth (1868–1968), Friedrich Gogarten (1887–1967) and Bultmann himself. Bultmann readily acknowledged the influence of Barth and Gogarten upon his own work, and it is appropriate to consider their contribution amongst the other major influences upon his thought.

Gogarten's essay 'Between the Times' (1920)[21] can be seen as marking the beginning of the movement. The title of the essay (in German, 'Zwischen den Zeiten') provided the name for the journal launched to promote the new theological trend. The presence and activity of God, Gogarten argued, cannot be perceived in the cause–effect continuum of this world. God is not accessible to the psychologist or the historian in terms of these disciplines. The study of history does not lead to God but only to human despair. A God who could be discerned by the eye of the historian would only be an idol. True religion occurs only when 'man's busyness ceases and God's activity begins'.[22] Religion is thus the crisis of all human culture rather than a phenomenon embedded in culture.

What we see in Gogarten's early writings is a search for a theology which is strong enough to challenge and to expose the gravity of the human situation. It is no accident that it was formulated in the aftermath of the horrors of the Great War. The older liberal theology had over-stressed the continuity between human achievement and divine revelation. What was now required was a theology, in the manner of Luther, which challenged and relativized every human work through the preaching of the cross of Christ.

The most celebrated writing of dialectical theology was undoubtedly the second edition of Karl Barth's commentary on the epistle to the Romans (1922). Passionately written, it challenged the deepest assumptions of liberal theology concerning God, human nature, the kingdom and the Church. Barth had been schooled in the tradition of liberal theology but a decisive break was precipitated in 1914 by the publication in Germany of an open letter supporting the Kaiser's war policy. The letter was signed by many of the leading theologians of the day including his teachers, Herrmann and Harnack. For Barth, this signalled not only political misjudgement but the failure of an entire theological tradition. He believed that the radical message of the Bible, which he had struggled to preach Sunday by Sunday in the Swiss village of Safenwil, was being silenced by liberal theology. An alternative approach had to be found. Barth later said that he was like a man who, stumbling blindly in a church tower, had clutched at the nearest rope only to discover that it was the bell-rope and that he had awakened the entire countryside.

The message of Barth's *Romans* was that the Bible witnessed above all else to 'the infinite qualitative distinction' between God and the world. The strange, radically other, and peculiar character of God had been eclipsed by liberalism. The term 'dialectical' referred to the sharp contrast between God and the world. This dialectic was not that of Hegel in which every contradiction is taken up and resolved in an inevitable synthesis. It resembled more the dialectic of Kierkegaard, the nineteenth-century Danish philosopher, in which the distinction between God and the world was enduring. There could be no thinking away or ignoring of this yawning chasm. *Romans* emphasized over and over again the Lordship of God and the brokenness of humanity. Where liberal theology saw continuity and progression, Barth could only find discontinuity and disruption. The Bible witnessed to the sovereign judgement of God and the otherwise hopeless predicament of human beings. Even the very style in which Barth wrote emphasized, through the use of violent juxtaposition, the theological rebellion that was taking place in his work.

The central axiom of Paul's epistle, according to Barth, is that the gospel of God does not arise from the world of human experience and possibility. It is a message that comes from above and beyond. Its coming both brings judgement on all human endeavour and offers a gracious release. The theme of grace can never be divorced from the theme of judgement if it is to be properly understood.

> The Gospel is not a religious message to inform mankind of their divinity or to tell them how they may become divine. The Gospel proclaims a God utterly distinct from men. Salvation comes to them from Him, because they are, as men, incapable of knowing Him, and because they have no right to claim anything from him.[23]

The mode of knowledge in which this message is heard and received is that of faith. Faith is the necessary corollary of revelation. Yet faith is not a natural human disposition. God's presence is not apparent through historical survey or psychological analysis. As 'the impossible possibility' it can be discovered only through the miracle of faith. This faith involves conversion, repentance and rebirth. Without it, God's word remains concealed and unrecognizable.

Barth's perceived discontinuity between God and the world also involved a renewed appreciation of the doctrine of sin. His *Romans* is replete with quotations from the Reformers and Kierkegaard. The optimism of German liberalism now gives way to a more sober and sombre estimate of human nature. 'Is the doctrine of original sin . . . not the doctrine which, in the last resort, underlies the whole teaching of history?'[24] In line with this, there is a sustained attempt to unmask a range of human pretensions culminating in religion. Three areas of study, all precious to liberalism, are attacked with fearsome hostility. These are history, ethics and religion. The word of God is not to be found through the investigations of a historical scholar nor through the insights of a moral philosopher. Even religion itself is a phenomenon in which human beings try to conceal from themselves their true plight. In the midst of a fallen and dying existence, human beings seek consolation by clinging to religion with a 'bourgeois tenacity'. To this extent, Christian faith is set in sharp opposition to religion, which is seen as a work of the human spirit. While some found this an artificial and even dishonest distinction, it is clear that it represented for Barth an aggressive attack on an entire theological tradition. To this extent, his work recalled Calvin's doctrine of total depravity in which every human activity, including religion, is such that even our best is flawed.

The dominant image of God's revelation is of the event which 'cuts down vertically from above'. It does not arise naturally from the world below but is given miraculously and unexpectedly. It is the fire-alarm of a coming new world, a flash of lightning, an explosion leaving a crater, the eternal moment of crisis. This event is the cross of Christ which creates a crisis for all human experience and history. Through that crisis, and only through it, lies our salvation. The kingdom of God does not emerge from the processes of history but is given and perceived on the other side of the cross of Christ.

When Bultmann read the second edition of Barth's *Romans* he was convinced of its relevance and force. He wrote a sympathetic review of the book[25] which Barth later described as the most remarkable thing that had happened to it. Bultmann was apparently the first historical scholar of repute to receive the book enthusiastically. He perceived the book as a timely warning against the dangers of psychologism in religion and pantheism in history. These represented the tendencies to detect God through psychological analysis of religious experience or through the historical study of the gospels. Bultmann agreed with Barth that the gift of faith was necessary for God's revelation to be received. It was a revelation which came from beyond rather than from within the natural course of events. As such it could be apprehended only through faith. The revelation of God, moreover, was one in which innate human capacities were judged and found to be wanting. Paul's theology of the cross of Christ was one both of judgement and of grace, and this Barth had correctly perceived. Being a Christian was primarily a matter of hearing and receiving the message of the cross, rather than communing with the religious personality of Jesus or enrolling as a member of an ethical kingdom (both liberal constructions).

There thus came to pass a further influence upon Bultmann's thought which can be detected in all of his theological writings. Bultmann's review of *Romans* established a theological harmony between himself and Barth, although it was one that was to prove short-lived. Already in that review we see criticisms of Barth which were to prove decisive in the years ahead. For Bultmann, it was imperative to consider the nature of faith as an historical event in the life of the believer. This was the only way in which God's word could be understood and explored. Beyond the experience of faith, God is hidden from us. For Barth, however, this ultimately entailed a retreat into liberalism. The theological task could only be executed through first considering the object of faith. Perhaps the best way to describe the eventual divergence between Barth and Bultmann is to say that, while for Barth the primary task was to elucidate the *content* of what is believed (to do this Barth revitalized the study of Christian dogmatics), for Bultmann the task was to elucidate the *character* of belief (to do this Bultmann found in Heidegger's existentialism a useful tool). Their alliance in the 1920s however was crucial to the establishment of dialectical theology and it produced a fascinating life-long correspondence between two of the most significant figures of twentieth-century theology.[26] In retrospect, it is clear that Bultmann and Barth were embarked on different courses. While Barth saw his work as making a radical break with liberalism, Bultmann, by contrast, believed he was developing the theological tradition of Herrmann. He later wrote to Erich Foerster:

> I must frankly confess to you that the war was not a shattering experience for me. Of course, there were endless issues but not the war as such. It is clear to me, as I have maintained in numerous conversations, that what happens in war is not different from peacetime; a shipwreck, an act of meanness, as they occur daily, present to us exactly the same question as the mass of events in the war. I do not believe, therefore, that the war influenced my theology . . . On the question of the origin of our theology, I am of the opinion that the internal debate with the theology of our teachers plays an incomparably greater role than the experiences of the war or the reading of Dostoevsky.[27]

Bultmann's commitment to dialectical theology came, not through the trauma of the war, but through the conversation that was taking place within liberalism. Already in the 1920 essay, 'Ethical and mystical religion in primitive Christianity',[28] we see Bultmann's obvious dissatisfaction with the historical and theological conclusions of his teachers. Historical investigation cannot uncover a particular episode in time and make it normative for the expression of religion. This would only domesticate and distort the transcendent reality of God.

This development of Bultmann's thought is confirmed by the correspondence with Martin Rade, which followed the publication of this essay in *Die Christliche Welt*, an organ of liberal theology. In a letter dated 19 July 1920, Bultmann writes to Rade that the Jesus presented by Heitmüller and others is little more than a symbol of a cultural ideal.[29] The authentic historical Jesus is not available to us in this way, and, to that extent, liberal theology is untenable. Bultmann's turning towards dialectical theology is not therefore the consequence of a sudden, radical shift in his position around 1922. It is more the result of a sustained dialogue with the work of his teachers, and a sense of the shortcomings of their conclusions. As an ally of Barth and Gogarten, Bultmann is not setting out upon a new course, but is developing what he has already learnt from Wilhelm Herrmann.

> I perceive my position as an ally of Barth and Gogarten in no way as the crossing over to a new theology, but as the consistent continuation of what I have learned from Herrmann.[30]

Nonetheless we should not allow this to prevent us from recognizing the influence of Barth's early theology upon Bultmann. Bultmann's theological essays from 1924 onwards are more emphatic and decisive in their critique of liberalism. His language is more self-consciously dialectical in expressing the relationship of God's revelation to normative human experience. Bultmann's theology, which developed slowly from out of his work as a historical critic of the New Testament, found its clearest expression only after 1922 and the influence of Barth.[31]

In this chapter we have attempted to chart the background to Bultmann's thought. While this has been a wide-ranging tour it is nevertheless a necessary one. It is vital to understand the range of influences upon Bultmann, partly because his thought is multi-dimensional, but also because it must be understood as a development beyond the liberalism of the nineteenth and early twentieth centuries, yet a development in which many of the elements of liberalism were retained and revised. This will become apparent as we examine the different aspects of his work as a theologian and a biblical critic.

Notes

1 Useful studies of the period include Alisdair Heron, *A Century of Protestant Theology* (London, 1980); Claude Welch, *Protestant Thought In The Nineteenth Century* 1-2 (New Haven, 1972-85); Alister McGrath, *The Making of Modern German Christology* (Oxford, 1986).

2 *An Enquiry Concerning Human Understanding*, ed. L. A. Selby-Bigge (Oxford, 1975), section X, pp. 109–31.

3 The most succinct Enlightenment critique of the proofs is found in Hume's *Dialogues Concerning Natural Religion*, ed. H. D. Aitken (New York, 1978). Many of his arguments are reiterated in Kant's *Critique of Pure Reason*, ed. N. Kemp-Smith (London, 1929), pp. 500–24.

4 *The Christian Faith*, ed. H. R. Mackintosh and J. S. Stewart (Edinburgh, 1928), p. 12.

5 Ibid., section 15, p. 76.

6 *The Christian Doctrine of Justification and Reconciliation*, ed. H. R. Mackintosh and A. B. Macaulay (Edinburgh, 1900), p. 387.

7 Ibid., p. 25. For a discussion of Ritschl's Christology see James Richmond, *Ritschl: A Reappraisal* (London, 1978), ch. V, pp. 168–219.

8 'Der Begriff der Religion nach Hermann Cohen' in *Schriften zur Grundlegung der Theologie* II (Munich, 1967), p. 322.

9 Herrmann's theological epistemology is outlined in his famous essay 'Die Wirklichkeit Gottes'. His statement 'Of God we can only say what he does to us' (p. 314) was often quoted by Bultmann.

10 *The So-Called Historical Jesus and the Historic Biblical Christ*, ed. C. E. Braaten (Philadelphia, 1964), pp. 46ff.

11 'Half a century of theology: A review' in R. Morgan and M. Pye (eds), *Writings on Theology and Religion* (London, 1977), p. 71. For a discussion of Troeltsch's relationship to liberal Christology see Sarah Coakley, *Christ Without Absolutes* (Oxford, 1988), ch. 2, pp. 45–99.

12 'On the proof of the Spirit and of power' in *Lessing's Theological Writings*, ed. H. Chadwick (London, 1956), p. 55.

13 Ibid., p. 53.

14 Albert Schweitzer, *The Quest of the Historical Jesus* (London, 1911), p. 4.

15 Ibid., pp. 50–7.

16 Ibid., p. 192.

17 The Marcan Hypothesis of Weisse and others is discussed by Schweitzer, ibid., pp. 121–36.

18 Ibid., p. 329.

19 Ibid., pp. 237–40.

20 Bultmann, 'Die liberale Theologie und die jüngste theologische Bewegung' (1924); 'Liberal theology and the latest theological movement', FU, pp. 29–30. For a discussion of Bultmann's place in the history of religions school see Helmut Koester, 'Early Christianity from the perspective of the history of religions: Rudolf Bultmann's contribution' in Edward C. Hobbs (ed.), *Bultmann: Retrospect and*

Prospect (Philadelphia, 1985), pp. 59–74; and also Robert Morgan and John Barton, *Biblical Interpretation* (Oxford, 1988), ch. 4.

21 Extracts from this and other key writings in dialectical theology are translated in James Robinson (ed.), *The Beginnings of Dialectical Theology* (Atlanta, 1968).

22 Ibid., p. 286.

23 *The Epistle to the Romans* (2nd ed., trans. Edwyn Hoskyns; Oxford, 1933), p. 28.

24 Ibid., pp. 85–6.

25 'Karl Barth's Römerbrief in zweiter Auflage' (1922); *The Beginnings of Dialectical Theology*, pp. 100–20.

26 Translated in *Letters*.

27 'Brief an Erich Foerster' in Bernd Jaspert (ed.), *Rudolf Bultmanns Werk und Wirkung* (Darmstadt, 1984), pp. 73–4. The translation is my own.

28 'Ethische und mystische Religion im Urchristentum'; trans. in *The Beginnings of Dialectical Theology*, pp. 221–35.

29 Cited by Bernd Jaspert, 'Rudolf Bultmanns Wende von der liberalen zur dialektischen Theologie' in *Rudolf Bultmanns Werk und Wirkung*, p. 31.

30 Letter of 23 March 1926, cited by Jaspert, ibid., p. 42. The translation is my own.

31 The development of Bultmann's thought from his student years until 1920 is analysed by Martin Evang, *Rudolf Bultmann in seiner Frühzeit* (Tübingen, 1988).

3

The miracle of faith

The leading concept in Bultmann's theology is that of 'faith' (*Glaube*). Faith is presented as a rich and multi-dimensional theme, and informs his understanding of the doctrine of God, the person of Jesus Christ, word and sacrament, and Christian ethics. His description of faith is therefore an index to all the central issues in his theology and it is significant that his four-volume collection of essays is entitled *Faith and Understanding* (*Glauben und Verstehen*). In this chapter, we shall consider his description of faith in order to grasp the shape of his theology. This will provide us with an overview of the main features of his thought, and enable us to place in perspective the details, which we shall subsequently explore.

The denial of faith

Certain mediaeval theologians argued that our understanding of God proceeded according to a negative way, *via negativa*. The process of ascending to a true knowledge of God was achieved through understanding what God is not. Theological knowledge could be attained by perceiving that God is not corporeal, not limited to one spatial position, not an individual member of a general class, not subject to change and decay, etc. By this negative route in which all false images of God are discarded, the human mind can approach, though never capture, the mystery of God's being. An analogous *via negativa* occurs in Bultmann's treatment of the concept of faith. Throughout his writings, he points to what faith is not, so that by eliminating a series of false constructions we can approach its true

27

meaning. We shall trace this negative route to a proper understanding of faith.

According to Bultmann, much theology has been flawed through attempting to reduce God to one phenomenon amongst others in the stream of history.[1] As this happens faith is reduced to a belief in a historical theory. One example of this would be the notion that God is to be identified as the supernatural cause of certain historical events, e.g. the exodus from Egypt, a military victory, or the sudden healing of a disease. In such cases God is perceived as an agent who intervenes occasionally in the course of nature and history. This divine intervention can be perceived by anyone who surveys the past. For Bultmann, this is not faith but superstition. The modern historian works with a belief in the closed causal nexus of events. There is no room for God to intervene occasionally, and alleged cases of the miraculous can generally be explained in natural terms.

Another example of this misguided attempt to read off the presence of God from the stream of history can be seen in nineteenth-century liberal theology. Here God is no longer seen as a divine agent who intervenes occasionally in the causal continuum of history; rather he is discerned in the personalities who shape history. Above all others, Jesus is seen as manifesting in his personality the presence and activity of God. In the power of his religious psyche we see the Spirit of God active in human history. Bultmann rejects this as a 'pantheism of history'. It leads to the view that human personality is divine or is capable of manifesting the divine to the student of history. Faith in God has nothing to do with such historiography.

For Bultmann, there is no direct knowledge of God in the way that we have direct knowledge of sensible things or in the way that we can perceive that $2 + 2 = 4$. God is not available to us in a similiar mode to empirical experience or the propositions of mathematics and science. Any attempt to perceive God from a neutral or detached standpoint will inevitably result in distortion; God is not a given entity who lies at our disposal and who can be inspected critically by the scientist or the historian. God is known only in personal encounter, and never on our terms. Bultmann believed this to be one of the central insights of the dialectical theology of Gogarten and Barth. God is a subject who addresses us rather than an object under our control. The divine address can be heard and believed only in the moment of faith.

In similar fashion, Bultmann insists that faith must never be construed as assent to a world-view (*Weltanschauung*).[2] A world-view is an explanatory hypothesis which can be constructed and tested by an impartial investigator. In the case of the cosmological argument where God is postulated as the necessary first cause of the universe, we have the outline of a world-view which can be formulated by a philosopher or scientist. But, according to Bultmann, the character of God is now distorted. God is reduced to a principle within a system of thought, and faith has been assimilated to mere intellectual assent to a world-view. Bultmann even argues that the construction of a world-view is symptomatic of an ingrained desire to avoid responsibility for our human condition. By explaining our existence in terms of a world-view, we account for our existence by reference to conditions outside ourselves. In this way, we evade our responsibilities by seeking refuge in a false security. To this extent, the construction of a world-view is the very antithesis of faith. Faith must involve an encounter with God in which my whole being is determined and called into question.

A central notion in Bultmann's polemic against false constructions of faith is the notion of 'objectification'. The historian and the scientist are constantly engaged in the activity of objectifying. This occurs when the relevant data are assessed, and an explanatory theory is put forward which explains and classifies these data. Objectifying thus occurs when the investigator creates a model for understanding reality. While this is a perfectly legitimate procedure for a scientist or a historian, Bultmann considers that it is inappropriate for the theologian. To objectify (*objektivieren*) entails setting out a thesis which can be discussed and acknowledged in detachment from the reality in question. The results of such objectification are the fruits of human labour. But when objectifying patterns of thought intrude into theology faith is distorted. Faith involves commitment and obedience to a reality which calls one in question. There is no external vantage point from which this reality can be spoken of. There is no sense in which my confession of that reality is a creative human achievement. Thus the activity of objectifying is inimical to the practice of faith.

Throughout all of his writings the verb 'to objectify' and its cognates are used in this deprecatory sense.[3] It is crucial however to realize that this does not entail a denial of the 'objectivity' of God, in the sense in which we ordinarily use that word. Bultmann is not arguing that faith is purely subjective. On the contrary, his intention is the reverse. It is only by rescuing faith from the objectifying activity of human reason that the reality of God is safeguarded in theology. God as the Subject who encounters us can never be encapsulated by the objective constructions of human reason.

Bultmann sometimes speaks of God as the 'Wholly Other', an expression originally coined by Rudolf Otto, his colleague in Marburg. As 'Wholly Other' God cannot be known or controlled by the human mind as are other data of experience. God can be known only through self-revelation as the one who is distinct from the phenomena of nature and history.[4]

Christian theology has been bedevilled by attempts to objectify God and faith. A theology which is grounded upon a belief in the inerrancy of the words of Scripture has fallen into the trap of objectifying. It has reduced faith to a system which the mind can assent to in a detached manner. Similarly, to construe faith as the assent of the intellect to a series of ecclesiastical dogmas is also to objectify. It represents a failure to see that faith is primarily a critical encounter with God in which my whole being is called in question and changed. Here Bultmann remains close to Wilhelm Herrmann.

> The affirmation of faith in its relation to its object, to God, cannot be proved objectively. This is not a weakness of faith; it is its true strength, as my teacher Wilhelm Herrmann insisted. For if the relation between faith and God could be proved as the relation between subject and object in worldly situations can be proved, then He would be placed on the same level as the world, within which the demand for proof is legitimate.[5]

A further distinction that Bultmann employs to illustrate this point is the classical one between *fides quae creditur* and *fides qua creditur*.[6] According to this distinction, *fides quae creditur* (the faith which is believed) is the subject-matter of theology, while *fides qua creditur* (the faith by which one believes) is the giving of assent to the *fides quae creditur*. In this way the act of faith can only be understood as secondary to the content of faith. For Bultmann however this leads to a warping of the concept of faith. Here it has been reduced to an 'objective' system which the mind has to acknowledge as true. The system stands over against the human subject in a manner which obscures the irreducibly personal quality of faith. The theologian must recognize the primary importance of the act of faith (*fides qua creditur*) in which the believer is personally engaged by the word of God. At the same time, one must beware of committing the opposite error of making the act of faith itself the subject of psychological analysis. This would constitute the form of objectifying into which Schleiermacher's theology lapses. In order to avoid a false detachment, theology must itself be part of this act of faith. The theologian cannot stand outside the relationship in which he or she stands to God. The theological expression of faith is itself part of the movement of faith.

> Theology is nothing other than the reflective, methodical unfolding of the understanding of the word of God and of the self-understanding disclosed through this word and given in faith.[7]

Throughout his writings, Bultmann is preoccupied with the personal and inward character of faith which involves me as a person in the concrete, historical circumstances of my existence. The self-involving or existential character of faith must be laid bare by theology. The besetting temptation of the theologian is always to objectify in order to win a false security and respectability for faith.

In support of this analysis Bultmann often points to analogies from other areas of human experience. It is a pervasive feature of our existence that we only truly understand the meaning of an event when first we have had personal experience of it. We do not really understand what it means to fall in love, to be married, to have children and friends, to mourn, or to be faced with death until we have encountered these personally. No amount of reading books or formulating theories can be an adequate substitute. I can be instructed in theories about the grief process and talk to people who have been bereaved, but until I personally meet with grief I cannot truly understand it. Similarly I can meet with people who are terminally ill and even formulate a theology of dying, but until I myself am threatened by a doctor's diagnosis or by serving in the front line of an army I do not really understand what it means to face death. I can read poetry and novels about romance, but until I fall in love I have not really understood what love is. Understanding occurs only when these realities are encountered in the concrete circumstances of human existence. The formal awareness that takes place prior to personal experience is no substitute and should never be confused with true understanding. The same applies, *a fortiori*, to faith. In faith, my entire existence is called into question and set on an entirely new basis. This is something that affects every part of my being. It can only be understood from the inside and remains opaque to every external investigation.[8]

At this point it is worth registering a possible criticism of Bultmann. Since we are dealing with the fundamental orientation of his theology, what is said here will affect other aspects of his thought. It might be argued that Bultmann's disjoining of faith and 'objectivity' results in a false antithesis. While there is undoubtedly a personal, existential dimension to faith, which can be lost sight of in theology, this does not necessarily entail that faith has nothing whatsoever to do with a world-view. Could it not be the case that while the validity of the Christian world-view can only be perceived in faith, nonetheless, the believer is committed to formulating such a world-view in order to understand and express faith? Related to this is the further problem of how faith can ever come to expression in statements about God and the world without violating Bultmann's prohibition on objectivizing patterns of thought. Is Bultmann not in danger here of reducing faith to mere human self-description? If faith is truly an encounter with God, the believer can only express this in statements referring to God. How can I talk of God other than in propositions which commit me to a particular world-view? Philosophers sometimes describe the holding of a belief as a propositional attitude. Bultmann may be in danger of excluding propositional attitudes altogether from his understanding of faith. But is this possible if faith refers to a reality other than myself? Bultmann may have emphasized the inwardness and personal character of faith at too high a price. This is a question to which we shall return later.

The form and content of faith

God, as we have seen, is not a given entity like the objects of sensory experience. God does not lie at our disposal and cannot be spoken of in terms which are generally valid to the observer. Therefore if God is known to us it is through divine self-revelation. Such revelation can occur only in the context of a deeply personal encounter between God and the believer. The disclosure must be controlled from God's side and the only appropriate human response is one of commitment and obedience.

For Bultmann faith is the necessary corollary of revelation. It is not a natural phenomenon but is wholly unexpected and miraculous. It is the entry into human life of an event which is discontinuous with everything that precedes it. Yet it is an event which transforms human life in the most radical way.

Faith is never self-evident, natural; it is always miraculous. The belief that God is the Father and man is the child of God is not an insight which can be gained directly—it is not an insight at all.

On the contrary, it must be believed, ever and again, as the miraculous act of God.[9]

Since faith is never under my control it is something that must continually be appropriated. It is a recurring event rather than an intrinsic quality of being. Bultmann often speaks of the decisive moment (*Augenblick*) in which God's word is heard and faith is created. This occurrence is not something that is visible to the historian or the philosopher. It is an event which creates faith, and an event the meaning of which is known only within faith. Thus the revelation of God is wholly miraculous and cannot be detached from the act in which it is apprehended.

Faith, rather than involving intellectual assent to a series of propositions, is more appropriately characterized as a radically new mode of existence. It is a new way of being which determines everything within human experience. It creates a new understanding of God together with a new understanding of the self. The one can never be understood in isolation from the other. Since faith is the basic mode of being for the Christian we must understand everything in the Christian life as proceeding from it. Here Bultmann is close to Luther's Reformation principle of *sola fide* (by faith alone). Faith thus becomes a rich theological concept which embraces all the main aspects of the Christian life.

Faith as decision. The occurrence of faith is not a phenomenal experience which leaves the inward self unaffected. It must be freely grasped and must engage the depths of one's being. In the moment of faith I resolve to accept God's word and to allow it to determine my life. Faith genuinely qualifies my existence. It cannot be given to me by my parents, my church or my culture. Being a Christian is not a matter of being born into a Christian community or being brought up in the church. It is something that I must will for myself in the moment of freedom that grace makes possible. Here Bultmann reflects much of what Kierkegaard had to say about the leap of faith. It must be a passionate, inward venture in which a human being makes a free commitment to God.

Faith as confession. In the act of faith I turn towards the self-disclosing God. This turning towards God implies a renunciation of any attempt to depend upon myself. It is an acknowledgement that the meaning and resources of existence are to be found only in God. Faith is the recognition of the claim that God makes upon me. Any attempt to ignore or to stand outside that claim is sin. To take up a position of neutrality with respect to God represents an avoidance of the claim that is made upon one.[10] Faith thus entails a confession of every false and vain attempt to live from out of one's own resources. The opposite of faith is sin. 'Whatever does not proceed from faith is sin' (Rom 14:23).

Faith as obedience. As an act in which I freely acknowledge God's claim upon me faith must be characterized by obedience. It implies a readiness to be determined by God's word and to live accordingly. Its nature as obedience indicates that faith is not to be construed as an achievement which ranks alongside other human works. It is merely submission to God and therefore implies the abandonment of every attempt to be self-determining. The meaning of existence is given by God, rather than created by the human subject. As simple obedience faith represents the end of self-preoccupation, of an existence in which the self is the focus and norm.

Hitherto we have spoken of faith only in a formal way. The marks of decision, confession and obedience are largely formal characteristics that could be found in other faiths. It is not until we examine their relationship to what Bultmann perceives to be the material content of God's revelation that we can appreciate their significance. Christian faith is not merely a formal commitment but involves a knowledge of what is possible and necessary through Jesus Christ. In this respect, knowledge remains a vital component of faith.[11]

Revelation is related to the concept of the word of God. This word is contained in the New Testament and is taken up in the witness of the Church. Yet the revelation given thereby does not offer objective information about God. It is not a deposit which can be viewed by the spectator who is unwilling to allow his or her life to be challenged by it. God is revealed only insofar as God acts upon one and determines one's existence. Here Bultmann is fond of quoting Herrmann's dictum, 'Of God we can only tell what he does to us'.[12] The witness to the content of revelation does not violate Bultmann's claim that faith has nothing to do with a world-view (*Weltanschauung*). The word is at one and the same time a revelation both of myself and of God. It reveals both God's judgement and grace. It exposes sinful existence, and yet offers forgiveness and grace. Here the key doctrine for articulating revelation is the Pauline–Lutheran doctrine of justification.

The judgement of God exposes and condemns every human attempt at self-justification. In the letters of Paul, this is represented by the attitude of the zealous Jew who sought justification through observance of the Old Testament laws. In the teaching of Jesus, it is portrayed in the parable of the Pharisee and the publican (Luke 18:9-14). The need for recognition in the sight of others belongs to all human beings from childhood onwards. In itself this need is quite natural and proper, but it becomes corrupt when we think we can earn this recognition by our efforts and achievements. Love, friendship and respect cannot be coerced from other human beings. They can only be given freely. The same desire for recognition can be observed in religion where recognition (righteousness) before the highest court of appeal (God) is sought.[13] Yet the notion that I can merit or control the goodwill of God represents the deepest form of corruption since I thereby seek to exalt myself to the level of God.

While for Paul (as Bultmann interprets him) works-righteousness was epitomized by a legalistic adherence to the law, it can also take many other forms and is a fundamental human condition. It is manifested in the attitude of those who glory in and seek their *raison d'être* in the accumulation of wealth, the advancement of a career, the attainment of political power, in appearing sexually attractive, in belonging to a race, a family or a social grouping. In each of these instances some feature of God's creation has been perverted. Instead of being offered to God it has become the means by which human beings exalt themselves in the sight of others and in the presence of God. This is a denial of how things really are. It is a search for false comfort and security, an evasion of the inevitability of death, and a negation of divine grace.

The proclamation of the Church declares the forgiveness of God. I am justified not *because* of what I have done but *despite* it. As I acknowledge this in faith so my relationship to God changes radically. I discover myself to be accepted entirely on the basis of God's gracious action and I am released from the burden of having to justify myself. But how, it must be asked, is this act of justification effected by God? In what way is the event brought about and how is it recognizable?

Bultmann's answer is that justification is effected in the cross and resurrection of Jesus Christ. God's act of justifying the sinner is made possible through the death of Christ. The significance of Jesus is located neither in his teaching nor in his personality but only in his death. Because the Lord is also the crucified one this implies a condemnation of every human desire and achievement. The cross is the event in which all human self-sufficiency and endeavour are exposed as false and corrupt. Because God has spoken in the shame of the cross, the ways of the world are negated and undermined. 'God chose what is foolish in the world to shame the wise, God chose what is weak in the world to shame the strong' (1 Cor 1:27). The resurrection is also part of this same 'Christ event'. God's judgement upon the world through the cross of Christ is at the same time an offer of forgiveness. In submitting to this judgement we find ourselves forgiven and liberated. The cross represents the end of self-justification, but the resurrection implies forgiveness and freedom for those who 'take up the cross' in faith. Cross and resurrection must therefore be understood together and in the light of one another.[14]

Bultmann's understanding of the content of revelation is seen most clearly in his interpretation of Paul.[15] He argues that Paul is, for the most part, uninterested in the life of Jesus prior to the crucifixion and makes little mention of it in his letters. He concentrates upon the death and resurrection of Jesus as the occurrence in which the believer is justified by grace alone. In this respect, Paul is not an innovator but is handing down the tradition which he received from others (1 Cor 11:23ff.; 1 Cor 15:3). The gospel is contained neither in a metaphysical theory about the person of Christ nor in the power of his teaching and example. Human existence is transformed simply by the power of the cross and resurrection. 'We preach Christ crucified, a stumbling block to Jews and folly to Gentiles, but to those who are called, both Jews and Greeks, Christ the power of God and the wisdom of God' (1 Cor 1:23–24).

We see here the harmony between Bultmann's theology and his exegesis. Faith, he insists, is not to be assimilated to objective information or a theological world-view. In Paul, God's revelation is not understood in terms of imparting propositional knowledge or communicating information. It is revelation only insofar as it is an event in which I am called into question and changed in my innermost being.

> We know about revelation because it belongs to our life. You cannot communicate a concept of revelation to someone in the way in which you can communicate to him that there are species of fish that bear their young alive or that there are carnivorous plants. There is no revelation in this sense. Rather if you speak to someone of revelation, you speak to him about his authentic life, in the conviction that revelation belongs to this life, just as do light and darkness and love and friendship.[16]

The importance of Jesus for faith resides neither in his teaching nor in his religious consciousness. Jesus is significant because in his death and resurrection God is decisively revealed to us. The consequence of this is that the quest of the historical Jesus is theologically unnecessary. It is of little concern to the theologian whether the historian can have access to the authentic sayings of Jesus or can peer into his psyche. The Christian faith proclaims the cross of Christ as the event in and by which we are saved. The life of Jesus prior to that moment is therefore of no theological interest. If New Testament criticism has shown that the inner life of Jesus is inaccessible, then Bultmann can respond that this only goes to show that the writers, in proclaiming the gospel, had no need to resort to the religious consciousness of Jesus. The focus of concern lies elsewhere.

> I often have the impression that my conservative New Testament colleagues feel very uncomfortable, for I see them perpetually engaged in salvage operations. I calmly let the fire burn, for I see that what is consumed is only the fanciful portraits of Life-of-Jesus theology, and that means nothing other than 'Christ after the flesh' . . . How things looked in the heart of Jesus I do not know and do not want to know.[17]

The meaning of Jesus Christ is expressed neither by the doctrine of the two natures nor by a traditional theory of the atonement. These represent attempts to reduce revelation to a deposit of information which can be assessed and transmitted objectively. Jesus is proclaimed only because he is the bearer of the cross which is the event by which God has chosen to save humankind. It is in this sense that Jesus can be spoken of as Lord and Saviour.

It is worth considering here Bultmann's comments on the Christological confession of the First Assembly of the World Council of Churches in Amsterdam (1948): '*The World Council of Churches is composed of Churches which acknowledge Jesus Christ as God and Saviour*'. Bultmann argues that when the New Testament makes statements about Jesus' divinity its primary intention is to express the belief that, in Jesus, God has acted decisively. Insofar as the New Testament lapses occasionally into objectivizing Jesus' divinity it is to be criticized in the light of its own central message. The significance of Jesus is functional rather than metaphysical. The formula 'Christ is God' cannot be understood in Chalcedonian terms of two natures in one person. It can only be understood as referring to the Christ event in which God acts for us.

> The formula 'Christ is God' is false in every sense in which God is understood as an entity which can be objectivized, whether it

is understood in an Arian or Nicene, an Orthodox or a Liberal sense. It is correct, if 'God' is understood here as the event of God's acting. But my question is, ought one not rather to avoid such formulae on account of misunderstanding and cheerfully content oneself with saying that he is the Word of God?[18]

We have seen that for Bultmann the revelation of God is the event of my justification. In it I am at once judged, forgiven and liberated. This is revealed in the cross and resurrection of Jesus which are really but two dimensions of the one reality. Yet still it will be asked how I know that the cross of Christ is the occasion of my salvation. How do I know that it is in this one death that God is revealed? How do I know that of all the crucifixions that took place under Pontius Pilate this one was for me? Bultmann's answer concerns the way in which this one event becomes the word of God.

The moment of faith

The death and resurrection of Christ become the saving event for me when they are preached and heard as such. This is the only way in which the truth of the gospel can be confirmed. It is proclaimed and it is received in faith. We can enquire no further than this. Bultmann's emphasis upon the proclaimed word reflects his Lutheran understanding of the way in which the gospel is communicated. The cross of Christ becomes God's revelation as it is preached in the Christian community and as it is appropriated in faith. The task of the preacher was one that Bultmann himself took seriously and he writes as one who is passionately convinced of the importance and necessity of Christian preaching.

We may well be amazed, but the concrete situation for the preacher actually is that when he goes up into the pulpit, a printed book lies before him. And that book must be the basis for his preaching, exactly as if it had 'fallen from heaven'.[19]

It would be wrong, however, to interpret Bultmann as claiming that the word was communicated only through the medium of the Sunday sermon from the pulpit. While this was important to him the word could also be communicated in other ways. It can occur through a private reading of the Scriptures, through the silent witness of another Christian, or through receiving the sacraments. The meaning of the sacraments is, in essence, similar to the meaning of preaching.

> Baptism and the Lord's Supper are only a special means of re-presenting the salvation-occurrence, which in general is re-presented in the word of preaching.[20]

Conversely, Bultmann can speak of the sacramental quality of preaching. It is a means of representing the past in such a way that the past becomes a present encounter with God in which the sinner is justified and set free.[21] Preaching and the Lord's Supper are both means of grace in which the miracle of faith can be repeated.

Yet how do I know that the preaching of the Cross of Christ is God's word to me? Philosophical critics of Bultmann have argued that he advocates a blind faith, a dangerous form of irrationalism in which belief is not subject to any checks or constraints. In the absence of any reasons being advanced for offering obedience to the word of the cross rather than to some other word Bultmann has been charged with obscurantism.[22] His response to this is that such a charge begs the question. He has already claimed that faith cannot be reduced to an objective world-view, and therefore the demand for proof in the manner of a historical or scientific hypothesis is wholly inappropriate. As soon as I seek to secure a proof of faith I have destroyed its character. I have attempted to stand outside faith and view it from a neutral standpoint. This is impossible.

> The word of proclamation encounters us as God's word, in relation to which we cannot raise the question of legitimation, but which rather asks us whether we are willing to believe it.[23]

Despite this response, a further criticism has been made by some of Bultmann's closest followers. While accepting that faith cannot be objectively proven they remain uneasy with his assertion that the account of the historical life of Jesus is largely irrelevant to the Christian proclamation. The reason why the cross of Christ, rather than someone else's cross, is proclaimed must surely be elucidated by reference to the circumstances leading up to the crucifixion. This is a task that the gospel writers were clearly engaged in and it is hard to see how we can preach Christ crucified and risen if we can say nothing else about him. This aspect of the faith–history problem has given rise to considerable debate amongst a group of Bultmann's pupils, and we shall examine it in more detail in the concluding chapter.

Before leaving this preliminary discussion of Bultmann's theology we should consider his response to the problem of the rival claims of other religions. This was an issue that surfaced in a lively, though somewhat ill-tempered, debate with the Swiss philosopher Karl Jaspers.[24] Jaspers argued that Bultmann remained a prisoner of an old-fashioned and illiberal orthodoxy in which the revelation of God was limited to a single episode in the past. A more enlightened view of the matter would be to recognize that God can reveal himself to the human spirit through a whole range of media. The Muslim and the Hindu have their own revelations through sacred writings other than the Christian Scriptures.

> Liberality . . . repudiates the idea of an exclusive truth formulated in a credo. It recognizes that the way to God is possible also without Christ, and that Asians can find it without the Bible.[25]

Bultmann responded by arguing that Jaspers had understood neither the New Testament nor the meaning of revelation. Wherever a person acknowledges in faith that God has spoken then that revelation becomes for them decisive and absolute. The appropriate response is one of obedience rather than groping elsewhere for alternative revelations. To this extent, the Christian is irrevocably committed to the absolute significance of the cross of Christ. Bultmann's response to Jaspers is very much the Lutheran 'here I stand, I can do no other'.

Yet, while this is the only possible attitude for the personal confession of faith, it is nonetheless possible, argues Bultmann, for the historian to compare and contrast the Christian religion with other religions. God's revelation can be distinguished from human responses to it. As an historical and cultural phenomenon, Christianity can be classified and criticized. In some respects it may emerge as superior and in others as inferior. The study of comparative religion is thus quite legitimate as an historical enterprise. This however is not to be confused with the standpoint of faith in which the word of God is confessed as absolute and unparalleled. When a person hears the message that God has judged, forgiven and liberated the world in Christ this becomes, for that person, the decisive and absolute revelation. To assess it by setting it alongside other revelations would again be a instance of 'objectivizing' and would lead to the destruction of the true character of faith.[26] While this distinction would not satisfy all Bultmann's critics (nor indeed some of his closest followers), it is nonetheless clear that it is a distinction which proceeds legitimately from the difference he perceives between faith and a world-view.

The imperative of faith

The miracle of faith is an event in the concrete, personal existence of the human subject. It is an event which transforms the being of the believer and makes an impact upon the practical and everyday concerns of the believer. This new mode of being made possible by faith has an inherent ethical dimension.

In becoming justified by God's grace alone the believer is set free from the compulsion to gain security by effort. This is a freedom not only *from* the past but also *for* the future. It is a freedom to live in accordance with God's will in the everyday, practical world. The moral life of the Christian is therefore characterized by obedience to God's word. Bultmann often speaks in this context of the relationship between the indicative and the imperative.[27] The indicative refers to what God has done and what the believer has become in faith. The imperative refers to the way in which the believer must live in order to remain faithful to this state of affairs. Consequently, the indicative of faith implies the imperative of Christian action. 'If we live by the Spirit, let us also walk by the Spirit' (Gal 5:25).

We see here the close relationship between faith and hope. In faith I am liberated from my past and set free to live for God in each new moment. The attitude of the believer towards the future is thus one of hope. The future is faced with trust and confidence in the knowledge that I stand secure in the love of God, and not in anything I may or may not achieve for myself. Obedience is therefore not a grim determination to defy the odds; it is marked by hope, joy and freedom in those who are the disciples of Christ.

In this life the believer is beset by paradox. Faith must still be lived out in a world which remains sinful and by people who are caught up in it. There is therefore an acute dialectical tension in the life of the Christian who remains *in* the world but not *of* it. The imperative of faith comes to people who remain imperfect and flawed, though forgiven and justified by God. The Christian life is dominated by the struggle to live in a sinful, fallen world in complete obedience to God's grace. It is lived in the knowledge that God's promise is certain yet still unfulfilled. Bultmann frequently cites 2 Corinthians 6:9f. in this connection:

. . . as unknown and yet well known, as dying and behold we live; as punished, and yet not killed; as sorrowful, yet always rejoicing; as poor, yet making many rich; as having nothing, and yet possessing everything.

When we enquire into the content of the imperative we can begin to see the close relationship between faith and love. For Bultmann, both hope and love are essential aspects of faith. The three theological virtues are but different dimensions of a single reality. The believer who is set free in faith is indebted to the love of God. It is God's love alone which forgives and liberates. Therefore to live in obedience to God is to live in obedience to love. The Christian is called to obey the love of God and therefore to love all those whom God loves.

Self-surrender through the cross means positively that the man who no longer wills to be for himself exists for others. Since what has been opened up to him in the cross is the liberating love of God, the love of Christ also compels him to serve his fellow men (2 Cor 5:14), and his faith is active in love (Gal 5:6).[28]

The Christian is one who is called to love others in obedience to the love of God. Yet what distinguishes the Christian imperative from other ethical imperatives, according to Bultmann, is not so much its content as its form. Love is owed by the Christian to others neither on a utilitarian basis nor as a means of self-realization. It is owed purely as obedience to the God who has demonstrated love in Christ. The ethical life of the Christian can only be understood in the context of faith.

The virtue of love is not itself the discovery of the Christian faith. Bultmann argues that it is present in the Old Testament, in rabbinic Judaism and even in paganism.[29] The New Testament itself recognizes this when it states that 'he who loves his neighbour has fulfilled the law' (Rom 13:8). For the Christian, moral conduct does not necessarily have a different content. Its difference lies in that it has the form of obedience to the love of God.[30] Bultmann believes that people may know that love is a moral imperative through conscience or a religious tradition other than the Christian one. What is distinctive in Christian faith is the way in which this imperative proceeds from the indicative of faith.

For Bultmann, there is no distinctively Christian ethical system in the sense of a code of precepts which will tell believers how they ought to act in particular circumstances. To look for such a code is again to yearn for a false security. How one should love another person cannot be determined by a preconceived set of rules, but can only be worked out afresh in the concrete circumstances in which the other person is encountered. The Christian must decide in each ethical situation what it means to love the other person and must trust that this will be made clear in the moment of choice.

> A man cannot control beforehand the possibilities upon which he must act; he cannot in the moment of decision fall back upon principles, upon a general ethical theory which can relieve him of responsibility for the decision; rather, every moment of decision is essentially new.[31]

Bultmann argues that Jesus himself did not present an ethical code which prescribed the right course of action in every set of circumstances.[32] The emphasis in his teaching is generally on the form of the ethical imperative as complete obedience to the judgement and mercy of God. Obedience for Jesus is not blind obedience to the precepts of Judaism but is a matter of personally submitting oneself without reserve to God in the particular moment of choice. In one set of circumstances this may imply the indissolubility of the marriage bond (Luke 16:18), while in another it may imply readiness to renounce the ties of family life (Luke 14:26).

Since the life of faith is inextricably personal there is no such thing as a system of Christian ethics. The virtue of love is apparent in different ethical systems and, in any case, a system which preempted the need for the discovery of truth in each particular set of circumstances would represent an abrogation of true decision. Equally, there is no such thing as a Christian social or political programme in the sense of a blueprint which must be applied in all situations. The Christian has a responsibility to make political and social judgements in obedience to God, but these can only be worked out in the time and place in which we find ourselves.[33] However, we might ask whether this sharp distinction between the form and content of Christian ethics can actually be sustained in practice.

Is it possible to speak about obedience to the sovereign love of the Creator God revealed in Christ, while at the same time denying that there is any specifically Christian content to moral values? The beliefs we hold about human nature and the purposes of God must surely infect the values to which we are committed. The question of what is owed to another person (the question of justice) must be determined by one's theological commitments. Bultmann's understanding of the necessary improvisation involved in personal relationships needs to be matched by an account of how Christians are to determine the basic principles of justice which inform their social and political thinking. His disjunction between the form and content of ethical demands seems too reminiscent of the post-Enlightenment split between fact and value. In practice, as we shall now see, he was unable to sustain this disjunction between the form and content of ethics.

Excursus: Bultmann and National Socialism

Bultmann's work as a whole cannot be considered overtly political, particularly in comparision with recent liberation theology. His theology is marked by the liberal emphasis upon the freedom of the individual and, consequently, he tends to regard the human self independently of social, economic and political forces. Nonetheless, he believed that theologians and preachers are called upon to confess the Christian faith in response to the concrete, existential conditions they encounter. Of all the significant political occurrences in his lifetime the momentous events in Germany during the 1930s called for such a response.

The ideology of the National Socialist Party, which came to power in 1932, was based upon the concept of race. Race was held to be the determining factor in all historical events, and the supreme Aryan race was capable of unrivalled intellectual and spiritual achievement. In particular, the German race was destined to play a special role in the history of the world although their efforts had been impeded by the Jews. Anti-Semitism was thus embedded in the ideology of Nazism.

The same year marked the founding of the 'Faith Movement of German Christians', an organization that sought to give the ideology of National Socialism a Christian dimension. The theology of the German Christians claimed that the separate identity of races and nations was ordained by God and, consequently, had to be preserved. The Christian had a duty before God to preserve the purity of the German race and in particular to prevent marriage between Germans and Jews.

We see in race, folk, and nation, orders of existence granted and entrusted to us by God. God's law for us is that we look to the

44

preservation of these orders. Consequently miscegenation is to be opposed. . . . In the mission to the Jews we perceive a grave danger to our nationality. It is an entrance gate for alien blood into our body politic.[34]

In 1933 Hitler was appointed Chancellor and a series of draconian measures, which quickly transformed the shape of German society, were soon implemented. It is easy looking back with the benefit of hindsight to perceive the implications of these events together with the aims of Hitler. Yet in the rapidly changing economic and political circumstances of Germany between the wars it was much harder to discern what was happening. At the start of the semester of that year Bultmann delivered a lecture with rare political overtones on 'The task of theology in the present situation'.[35] Here he attacked, cautiously though clearly, some of the trends taking place at that time. His criticism of the German Christians is unmistakable. The orders of family, nation and state may indeed be the gifts of God, but such is the nature of human sinfulness that they become ambivalent signs of God's will. The gospel exposes the way in which these orders have become corrupt instruments in human hands. The judgement of the cross upon the present and the past reveals that God's purposes can only be known from the perspective of the gospel. The orders of race, nation and state must therefore be subject to the control of God's word given in Jesus Christ alone.

Only he who knows the transcendent God who speaks his word of love to the world in Christ is able to extricate himself from this sinful world and to achieve a perspective from which the world's ordinances can really be known as ordinances of creation.[36]

In the same essay, Bultmann also attacked the anti-Semitism inherent in National Socialism. The command to love one's neighbour, and the nature of the Church as a community in which all human distinctions are irrelevant and therefore transcended—these represent a Christian condemnation of discrimination on grounds of race. Later in 1933, the theological faculty of Marburg University criticized a decree of the Church of the Old Prussian Union requiring all ecclesiastical appointees to give unqualified support to the State and to be, along with their wives, of Aryan extraction. Bultmann, the leading author of this Marburg response, published shortly afterwards a brief essay on the same subject.[37] In it he asserted that the Church cannot recognize anything other than complete unity between Jewish and non-Jewish Christians, and that it has the constant task of maintaining a critical distance from the activities of the State.

> The Church must abandon nothing of its proclamation which places even the national consciousness (*Volksbewusstsein*) under the criticism of the Word of God. If the national consciousness resists this criticism then it becomes the consciousness of an unchristian people who have forgotten their determination by God. Only under this criticism of the Word of God and in constant tension with it can a true national consciousness prosper in respecting its limits as well as its worth and task. The Church must not yield one step from this position if it wishes to remain true to its Lord.[38]

We see in this essay a close theological affinity with the Declaration of the Synod of Barmen in 1934.

> Jesus Christ, as he is attested for us in Holy Scripture, is the one Word of God which we have to hear and which we have to trust and obey in life and in death.[39]

The Synod of Barmen, representing the Confessing Church, was the finest collective example of the Church's resistance to National Socialism. Bultmann was a signatory of the Barmen Declaration and a member of the Confessing Church, as was his close friend and colleague at Marburg, Hans von Soden. We shall see in Chapter 6 how Bultmann's original demythologizing essay of 1941 was originally part of a discussion that took place in the Confessing Church.

It was probably Bultmann's commitment to dialectical theology which enabled him to stand firm as a theologian against the ideology of National Socialism. God, he insisted, is never revealed in the events, institutions or philosophies of history. Any attempt to reduce God to this level falls into the trap of objectification. God is not a datum of human experience but is only revealed through the word of the cross. This basis to his theology enabled him to resist any attempt to reduce theology to a theory of race or to a political cult. It provided him with an implicit political critique of every world-view.[40]

On the other hand, we may question whether in the actual

moment of political judgement Bultmann was able to separate the form from the content of Christian ethics. As we have seen, he claims that there is no distinctively Christian ethic; it is only the form of the ethical demand which is distinctive in Christian faith. He thus implies that the content of ethical judgements can be known on some other basis. Yet, significantly, when criticizing the theology and morals of the German Christians he appeals to the material content of Christian revelation. The gospel exposes human sin everywhere; it relativizes differences of race and culture; it reveals the imperative of love for each and every individual human being. It now appears that the content of Christian ethical and political judgements is being derived from the judgement and mercy of God as these are revealed in the gospel. Thus the content as much as the form of Christian values is dependent upon revelation. The Christian in formulating political and moral judgements must do so on the basis of Scripture and theology. Ironically, Bultmann's specific ethical statements suggest a weakness in his theory.

We have seen how Bultmann was prepared to make political and moral judgements on the basis of his theology. Indeed he regarded the events of the 1930s as a crisis not only for Germany but for the Christian faith itself. It was here being tested for its ability to speak critically and authentically to the world.[41] If Bultmann was not amongst the leaders and most prominent spokesmen for the Christian faith in the German Church struggle, it is nonetheless true that his theology remained uncompromised during that time. Walter Schmithals has said of Bultmann's essays and sermons from that period:

> Such words sound easy enough today. In their time they were brave words. If there are any theologians in our country who can look back without shame to what they said and wrote in 1933 and afterwards, Rudolf Bultmann is among them.[42]

Notes

1 E.g. 'Die liberale Theologie und die jüngste theologische Bewegung' (1924); 'Liberal theology and the latest theological movement', FU, pp. 28–52.

2 Cf. 'Die Krisis des Glaubens' (1931); 'The crisis in belief', EPT, pp. 1–21.

3 For an important study of the philosophical and theological roots of

this notion see Roger Johnson, *The Origins of Demythologising* (Leiden, 1974).

4 E.g. the important essay 'Welchen Sinn hat es, von Gott zu reden?'; 'What does it mean to speak of God?', FU, p. 56. Extracts from this and other key writings of Bultmann are found in R. Johnson (ed.), *Rudolf Bultmann—Interpreting Faith For the Modern Era* (London, 1987).

5 JCM, p. 72.

6 Cf. 'Zur Frage der Christologie' (1927); 'On the question of Christology', FU, pp. 117ff.

7 Cf. 'Theologie als Wissenschaft' (1941): 'Theology as science', NTM, p. 54.

8 Cf. *Der Begriff der Offenbarung* (Tübingen, 1929); 'The concept of revelation in the New Testament', EF, p. 68.

9 'Liberal theology and the latest theological movement', p. 47.

10 This is explored by Kierkegaard in his treatment of Abraham in *Fear and Trembling* (Princeton, 1983).

11 'What does it mean to speak of God?', pp. 54ff.

12 'Die Wirklichkeit Gottes' in *Schriften zur Grundlegung der Theologie* II (Munich, 1967), p. 314.

13 This is explored in 'Gnade und Freiheit' (1948); 'Grace and Freedom', EPT, pp. 168–81.

14 Cf. 'Jesus und Paulus' (1936); 'Jesus and Paul', EF, p. 234.

15 A summary of Bultmann's interpretation of Paul is found in the essay 'Paulus'; 'Paul', EF, pp. 130–72.

16 'The concept of revelation in the New Testament', p. 68.

17 'On the question of Christology', p. 132.

18 'Das christologische Bekenntnis des Ökumenischen Rates' (1951); 'The Christological confession of the World Council of Churches', EPT, pp. 273–90.

19 'On the question of Christology', p. 131. Although never ordained, Bultmann was a committed preacher. Selections of his sermons are published in *Marburger Predigten* (Tübingen, 1956; *This World and the Beyond*, London, 1960) and *Das Verkündigte Wort* (Tübingen, 1984). The significance of many of his earliest sermons for understanding the development of his theology is demonstrated by Martin Evang, *Rudolf Bultmann in seiner Frühzeit* (Tübingen, 1988), pp. 133–75.

20 'Jesus and Paul', p. 238.

21 'Neues Testament und Mythologie' (1941); 'New Testament and mythology', NTM, pp. 34–5.

22 E.g. Karl Jaspers, 'Myth and religion', K & M II, pp. 133–80; Ronald Hepburn, 'Demythologising and the problem of validity' in A. Flew and A. MacIntyre (eds), *New Essays in Philosophical Theology* (London, 1955), pp. 227–42.

23 'New Testament and mythology', p. 39.

24 K & M II, pp. 133–94.

25 Ibid., p. 171.

26 Ibid., pp. 193–4.

27 E.g. TNT II, pp. 80ff.

28 'Jesus and Paul', p. 237.

29 *Jesus*, pp. 110ff.

30 'Das Problem der Ethik bei Paulus' (1924); Ex, p. 51.

31 *Jesus*, p. 85. Cf. the sermon preached in June 1941 at the time of the German invasion of Russia: *This World and Beyond*, pp. 143–54.

32 *Jesus*, ch. 3, pp. 57–132.

33 Cf. 'Humanismus und Christentum' (1948); 'Humanism and Christianity', EPT, pp. 151–67.

34 'The guiding principles of the Faith Movement of the German Christians' (6 June 1932); trans. in A.C. Cochrane, *The Church's Confession Under Hitler* (Pittsburgh, 1976), pp. 222–3. For a general guide to this period see Klaus Scholder, *The Churches and the Third Reich* I and II (London, 1987–89).

35 'Die Aufgabe der Theologie in der gegenwärtigen Situation'; 'The task of theology in the present situation', EF, pp. 186–95.

36 Ibid., p. 191.

37 Both 'Gutachten der Theologischen Fakultät der Universität Marburg' and 'Der Arier-Paragraph im Raume der Kirche' are published in *Theologische Blätter* (1933), cols 289–94, 359–70.

38 Ibid., col. 368. The translation is my own.

39 Cochrane, p. 239.

40 This can be seen in TE, p. 8 or in the 1935 sermon on Acts 17:22–32: *This World and the Beyond*, pp. 1–13. Bultmann originally sent the sermon to Barth for publication in *Theologische Existenz Heute*, a journal instituted to promote theological opposition to National Socialism. Cf. *Letters*, pp. 82ff.

41 'The task of theology in the present situation', p. 195.

42 *An Introduction to the Theology of Rudolf Bultmann* (London, 1968), p. 299.

4

The hermeneutical task

We have seen already the extent to which Bultmann is at once a New Testament critic and a theologian. His concern is both to pursue vigorously the historical criticism of the New Testament that had been developed in the nineteenth and early twentieth centuries, and yet also to present a theological interpretation of Scripture which is faithful to the preaching of the Church.

A comprehensive interpretation of the New Testament cannot end with historical criticism. The theological message must be understood, interpreted and proclaimed. Only when this occurs has the interpreter understood the intention of the writers and the subject matter of their writings. However, before looking in detail at Bultmann's theological exegesis, it is necessary to examine the principles that inform his interpretation. Without a clear understanding of these his interpretation at times will seem arbitrary and implausible.

The hermeneutical tradition

Hermeneutics is the science of the interpretation of written texts. Traditionally it referred to the rules governing grammatical forms and individual terms. By mastering these rules it became possible to translate and to interpret an ancient text. In this sense, 'hermeneutics' is restricted to the principles informing philology. In the writings of Schleiermacher, however, the term 'hermeneutics' is broadened in scope and this becomes the point of departure for modern theories. For Schleiermacher, interpretation cannot be exhausted merely by the rules of grammar. In order to understand a text we must perceive it as a moment in the life of its writer. We must understand the thoughts and feelings of the writer as they come to expression in the text. This requires not grammatical interpretation but psychological interpretation.[1] Only by 'divining' the psychological meaning embodied in the text can the interpreter come to understand what is being said. This task of psychological interpretation, therefore, requires empathy and intuition. This does not involve a psychoanalysis of the writer so much as the divination of the thought that is brought to expression in the text.[2]

The key concept of the 'hermeneutical circle' first comes to prominence in the work of Schleiermacher. The circular process of interpretation can be seen in at least two respects. Firstly, any text must be interpreted by understanding the parts in the light of the whole, and the whole in the light of the parts. Thus, whether the text be a Shakespeare play or a newspaper report on last night's football match, interpretation involves a constant trafficking between parts and whole. Our understanding of a soliloquy or a headline is conditioned by our understanding of what the meaning of the whole text is. At the same time, our understanding of the whole can only be arrived at through an interpretation of the parts. There is thus an inevitable circularity in any process of interpretation. Secondly, the meaning of the text can only be grasped where the text and the writer share something in common. A text about love or war can only be grasped where the interpreter already has some prior understanding of love and war and therefore can divine what the text is about. Yet the text may affect and change the interpreter's understanding of the subject and here again there is a circular process in the act of interpretation. It is through my preliminary knowledge of the subject that I read the text, yet the text may alter this preliminary knowledge. It is important to note that this is not a viciously circular procedure in which the interpreter merely reads out of the text what has been read in. The presuppositions that govern the interpretation can themselves be modified and transformed in the interpretive act. For this reason, the image of the hermeneutical *spiral* has sometimes been preferred to that of the circle. Nonetheless, the point remains that without some prior understanding on the part of the enquirer the meaning of the text cannot be comprehended.

For most of the nineteenth century Schleiermacher's work on hermeneutics was not developed. It was not until the philosophy of Wilhelm Dilthey (1833–1911) that many of his insights were recognized. Dilthey, moreover, continued the process by which the scope of hermeneutics was extended. It now had to be seen as the foundation for all the *Geisteswissenschaften*—the humanities and the social sciences. Drawing a contrast between the natural and the human sciences, Dilthey argued that understanding a text requires a comprehension of the total life experience embodied therein. This can only occur on the basis of one's own life experience which provides an entry into the world of the text. Whereas the natural sciences are engaged in explaining, the human sciences aspire to understanding. The personal involvement of the interpreter is therefore far greater than in natural science.

> [I]t is through the process of understanding that life in its depths is made clear to itself, and on the other hand we understand ourselves and others only when we transfer our own lived experience into every kind of expression of our own and other people's life. Thus everywhere the relation between lived experience, expression, and understanding is the proper procedure by which mankind as an object in the human studies exists for us.[3]

Dilthey's emphasis on the concrete, lived experience of the interpreter as the prior condition of interpretation both extends Schleiermacher's hermeneutics and anticipates the further development we find in Heidegger. It is only in the particular and personal moments of experience that meaning can be discerned. Only on the basis of a life relation to the subject matter of the text can the interpreter arrive at a genuine understanding. In this respect, a proper conception of the historicity (*Geschichtlichkeit*) of human existence is crucial for interpretation.[4] It is only from within a certain historical situation that a text can be interpreted and understood. The text itself belongs to another person's history, and understanding that text may enable interpreters to reach a deeper understanding of their own historical existence. As we shall see, it is this ability of a text to determine the historical existence of the interpreter that is central to Bultmann's theological understanding of the New Testament.

Bultmann's approach to hermeneutics

Bultmann sees his approach as standing in the tradition of Schleiermacher and Dilthey, yet he is aware of certain difficulties in their procedure. The emphasis upon psychological interpretation in

Schleiermacher's thought is to a large extent valid; it indicates that understanding is not achieved merely by grammatical interpretation. But it is not a necessary condition for all interpretation. In many cases, the psychological state of the writer may be quite irrelevant to the interpretive task. In the case of a mathematical text or the inscription on an ancient coin the psychological processes of the writer are probably of no interest to the interpreter. In view of this, it is important to recognize that the act of interpretation is conditioned by the particular interest of the interpreter.[5] The questions that are put to the text will have a bearing upon the answers that are discovered there. This is only possible where there is a shared interest between writer and interpreter, as Dilthey had already shown. Both writer and interpreter must inhabit a common world in which they associate in similar ways with objects and people. Without this presumption of a common context, understanding cannot take place.

> Only he who lives in a state and in a society can understand the political and social phenomena of the past and their history, just as only he who has a relation to music can understand a text that deals with music.[6]

Different types of interpretation are determined by different objectives. The ancient historian, the art critic and the psychoanalyst will each approach a text with a specific set of questions which will shape the subsequent interpretation.[7] In addition to these types of interpretation, there is a further possibility which might be labelled 'existential interpretation'. This refers to the way in which a text can express an understanding of the most fundamental possibilities of existence for a human being living under historical conditions. Since the ultimate questions of human existence beset both writer and interpreter there is a shared horizon which makes existential understanding possible. In principle, any text can be read existentially, i.e. as expressing some possibility of human existence. Bultmann acknowledges however that the texts that most readily lend themselves to such interpretation are those of philosophy, religion and literature.[8] In this respect, his hermeneutical strategy is not directed exclusively at the Bible although this is clearly where his dominant concern lies.

Like Dilthey (and Heidegger) Bultmann constantly emphasizes the importance of the historical nature of human existence. It is only by participation and self-involvement in concrete existence that understanding can take place. Existential interpretation cannot occur by way of neutral detachment or cold analysis. It is only when interpreters are engaged personally with the basic questions of their existence that existential understanding can occur. One consequence of this is that understanding must be won afresh by every interpreter from within that interpreter's situation. Interpretation is never complete but must be undertaken again and again in each generation.[9] For Bultmann, this insistence upon the 'subjective' interests of the interpreter does not result in arbitrary or capricious exegesis. On the contrary, the subjectivity of the interpreter is the only route to a properly 'objective' interpretation. It is only by allowing the text to confront oneself existentially that it can reveal its deepest character.

> The 'most subjective' interpretation is the 'most objective', because the only person who is able to hear the claim of the text is the person who is moved by the question of his or her own existence.[10]

We can now get into a position to view some of the more technical concepts that are employed by Bultmann in his hermeneutical theory.

(a) The *preunderstanding* (*Vorverständnis*) refers to the questions and concerns that the interpreter brings to the text and which determine the shape of the interpretation. Every interpretation is moved by some preunderstanding and, in the case of existential interpretation, the most fundamental questions of existence must be raised in one form or another. To formulate these questions the theologian must inevitably have recourse to the work of philosophy. For Bultmann this is unavoidable since every theology must employ concepts which describe human existence; we shall see presently how this convinced him of the usefulness of Heidegger's philosophy for theological interpretation.

In an existential preunderstanding the question of God is alive in various ways. It is the question which preoccupies every enquirer and which makes possible a proper theological interpretation of the New Testament. In the same way as friendship can be recognized as a possibility before being encountered existentially, so it is with the apprehension of the word of God. It is not that I already know prior to reading the New Testament what is revealed there. It is simply that I cannot hear it unless I am moved by the appropriate questions. It is in this sense only that Bultmann speaks of a natural theology which is a preamble to and a condition for the revelation of God.

54

Unless our existence were moved (consciously or unconsciously) by the question about God in the sense of Augustine's 'Thou hast made us for thyself, and our heart is restless until it rests in thee', we would not be able to recognize God as God in any revelation. There is an existential knowledge of God present and alive in human existence in the question about 'happiness' or 'salvation' or about the meaning of the authenticity of our own existence.[11]

(b) The *hermeneutical circle* is directly related to the necessity of preunderstanding. Interpretation can only commence on the basis of a prior understanding of the subject matter. The text must be interpreted in the light of some preunderstanding, yet, as we have seen, this preunderstanding itself can be changed and transformed by the text. It is for this last reason that Bultmann claims that the interpreter does not merely read out of the text what is fed in.

The point, then, is not to eliminate the preunderstanding but to risk it, to raise it to the level of consciousness, and to test it critically in understanding the text.[12]

Another facet of the circularity of interpretation is the way in which the interpreter's conception of the overall nature of the subject matter controls the interpretation of the various parts of the text. It is only in the light of some conception of the main meaning of the text that the individual parts can be understood. This phenomenon is referred to as *Sachkritik* by Bultmann. This phrase is difficult to capture in English although it is sometimes rendered by 'content-criticism'. It refers to the manner in which an interpretation is controlled by an overall understanding of what the text is saying. The interpreter must judge what the writer's overall meaning is and assess what is said in the light of what is meant.

The character of this objective exegesis (*Sachexegese*) is even more exactly determined by the fact that an objective critique (*Sachkritik*) of it is both possible and necessary. . . . The objective criticism (*Sachkritik*) called for in objective exegesis (*Sachexegese*) can establish its standard only through the object (*Sache*) opened up by the text over which it has no control.[13]

In order to understand some important features of Bultmann's exegesis, it is necessary to recognize the validity of *Sachkritik*. It will enable Bultmann to establish what is essential to a writer's intention and what is inessential, and therefore to make a critical judgement on the meaning of the text. *Sachkritik* is not a new phenomenon; it has often been pointed out that Luther was working with a formally similar notion when he asserted that the letter of James was of straw by comparison with the letters of Paul. His conception of the true meaning of the Gospel enabled him to criticize parts of the New Testament where this was lost sight of.[14] There are of course dangers inherent in the procedure of *Sachkritik* which may lead to violence being done to the text. If prejudices cause one to disregard as inessential much that is vital to the meaning of the text, then it is clearly being misinterpreted. Nonetheless the proper response to this is not to eschew *Sachkritik* but to point to the necessary relation between whole and parts. If too many individual parts conflict with the reality of the whole then the latter must be revised. The hermeneutical circle can in this way expose and reshape a deficient preunderstanding.

It is interesting in the light of recent hermeneutical discussion, particularly deconstructionism, to note how important the nature of authorial intention is for Bultmann. The conscious intention of the writer to give expression to an understanding of human existence is what, for Bultmann, controls the meaning of the text. By linking meaning to authorial intention, definite limits are set upon the interpretation of the text, and the possibility of a single, determinate meaning emerges. This is conditioned by Bultmann's belief that the fundamental possibilities of existence remain the same across human history and are not relative to a particular culture or epoch. This contrasts sharply with the apparent relativism and almost total fluidity of some recent hermeneutical strategies.[15]

(d) The technical distinction between *Historie* and *Geschichte* is also employed by Bultmann to indicate the nature of existential interpretation. This distinction is one he inherits largely from Martin Kähler and it is connected with his insistence upon the historicity (*Geschichtlichkeit*) of human existence. Unfortunately, it is difficult to capture the distinction in English since both words are translated as 'history'. *Historie* refers to the activity of scientific history in which the events of the past are studied and reconstructed. It is concerned with dates, places, battles, personalities, social, economic and political forces etc. *Geschichte*, on the other hand, refers to that dimension of history which challenges and transforms human existence. In Bultmann's theology, the paradigm example of this is the cross of Christ. As a datable event under the rule of Pontius Pilate it is a *historisch* event which is accessible to scientific study. Yet it is also a *geschichtlich* event by which existence before God is set on an entirely new basis. When taken up in faith the crucifixion becomes not only *Historie* but *Geschichte* also. As it confronts my own historical (*geschichtlich*) existence it becomes alive as *Geschichte*.[16]

It is by now abundantly clear that the task of interpretation is not exhausted by historical (*historisch*) criticism. For Bultmann a text, like the letter to the Romans, can only be properly understood when it has been existentially interpreted. It is only as the new possibility of existence under faith is grasped that Paul's meaning is apprehended. This however is not to deny the validity of historical criticism. Indeed, the existential meaning must be brought to light by distinguishing it from those aspects of Paul's thought which merely reflect the times and circumstances in which he was writing. Thus historical and existential interpretation complement one another insofar as the historical task can actually serve and illuminate the existential task. (As we shall see this is axiomatic to Bultmann's demythologizing programme.) There is a sense in which interpreters must respect their historical distance from the text, otherwise an archaic conceptuality may be mistaken for an understanding of human existence that is authentic across space and time.

This last point was a perpetually disputed issue between Barth and Bultmann. Barth had written in the preface to the second edition of his *Römerbrief*:

> Calvin, having first established what stands in the text, sets himself to re-think the whole material and to wrestle with it, till the walls which separate the sixteenth century from the first become transparent! Paul speaks, and the man of the sixteenth century hears. The conversation between the original record and the reader moves round the subject matter, until a distinction between yesterday and today becomes impossible.[17]

In reviewing this, Bultmann, although endorsing Barth's theological exegesis, insists that he has overlooked the extent to which Paul is a man of his times, and therefore bears the influences of a wide range of beliefs and practices which belong to the first century but not the twentieth. In order to determine the valid existential meaning of Paul's words it is necessary to discriminate the spirit of Christ from the other spirits that are alive in his writings. Failure to do this results in an exegesis which only faintly conceals an outmoded dogma of inerrancy. If theology is to avoid becoming enslaved to an discredited world-view, it is important that historical criticism is pursued in a relatively detached and scientific manner.[18]

It is necessary for the theologian to heed the work of the historical critic before presenting a theological interpretation of Scripture. The presupposition of historical enquiry is that the events of history form a causal continuum and can therefore be explained in terms of the context and circumstances under which they occurred.[19] This imposes the following constraints upon the interpretation of the New Testament:

1. The rules of grammar and translation that govern the language (i.e. Greek) in the time and place of writing must be observed.

2. The particular usage and style of the individual authors must be recognized.

3. The thought-world inhabited by the writers must be investigated in order to establish at what points the writers are being influenced by that thought-world. This is an important presupposition of the history of religions research.

4. The social circumstances that gave rise to the writing of the text must be explored in order to establish the *Sitz im Leben* of the documents. In the case of the New Testament this involves a study of the life, thought and worship of the early Christian community. This is an important presupposition of the history of traditions research.

These tasks of historical criticism must be prosecuted with all the energy that the critic can muster. Nonetheless this does not exhaust the interpretive act. Bultmann was profoundly dissatisfied with the scholarly work of many of his teachers which lacked anything resembling a theological interpretation, and which thus failed the subject matter of the texts under investigation. The writings of the New Testament proclaim the possibility of a new understanding of human existence and it is only when that possibility is realized by the interpreter that the meaning of the text is disclosed. The task of a theological interpretation of Scripture is to present the understanding of human life that arises from an existential encounter with the text. In Bultmann's writings, we see a growing understanding of theology as the scientific activity which provides a conceptual analysis of Christian existence. This is an activity which can be distinguished from Christian proclamation and confession, although it is dependent upon these.

The theme of New Testament theology is fundamentally the same as that of systematic theology: the conceptual explication of

Christian self-understanding, or of the eschatological occurrence, as it is attested in faith for faith. New Testament theology
explicates this occurrence by interpreting the New Testament in
such a way that the present urgency of the occurrence can be
understood. Systematic theology explicates this occurrence as it
is attested in the present in such a way that this present occurrence can be understood as the occurrence attested in the New
Testament.[20]

The understanding of existence presented in the New Testament
can only take place in the moment of faith. It is thus available only
to the interpreter who has heard the word of God in the text. To this
extent theological exegesis of Scripture is an ecclesial activity; it
takes place within the community of faith. Nonetheless theological
interpretation is scientific insofar as it attempts to conceptualize the
believer's understanding of existence. The theologian's task is to
present the existential understanding embedded in the proclamation
of the Scriptures and the Church.[21] To do this however theologians
must be equipped with philosophical concepts which will enable
them to articulate this new understanding of existence. This brings
us to a further prominent feature of Bultmann's hermeneutics,
namely, his appropriation of the philosophy of Martin Heidegger. It
is with Heidegger's philosophy that Bultmann's theology has been
most closely associated in the eyes of many critics, and it is necessary
to examine both that philosophy and Bultmann's controversial
adoption of it.

The philosophy of Heidegger

Martin Heidegger (1889–1976) is one of the most important and
difficult of twentieth-century philosophers. For the purposes of
understanding his influence upon Bultmann, it will be sufficient
to confine our attention to his *Being and Time*, which was first
published in 1927 when Heidegger was an associate professor of
philosophy in Marburg. Heidegger held this post from 1922 to 1928,
and during those years he and Bultmann collaborated together
by sharing seminars and engaging in dialogue with one another.
After Heidegger's departure for Freiburg in 1928 there was less
collaboration with Bultmann, and, perhaps as a consequence of
Heidegger's initial enthusiasm for the rise of National Socialism
in the 1930s, their relationship became somewhat strained.[22]
Nonetheless, the influence of Heidegger upon Bultmann was

enduring, as the dedication of *Faith and Understanding* demonstrates.[23]

The theme of Heidegger's philosophy is the question of Being. Heidegger believes that this is the most fundamental question of human inquiry but that it has been overlooked and lost sight of by most philosophers. His project is to re-open this ancient question but to do so he has to criticize other philosophical projects, including that of Descartes. In the *Discourse* and the *Meditations*, Descartes presents us with the picture of the self-conscious mental subject looking out at the world around it. This bare subject is in search of a rational proof of its own existence, the existence of God and the existence of the external world. This has been described as the turn to the subject in the history of Western thought. According to Heidegger this picture of the self is profoundly misguided. It involves several distortions, and consequently obscures rather than illuminates the question of Being.

Kant once remarked that it was a scandal that philosophy could provide no proof for the existence of the external world. Heidegger remarks that the real scandal is that such proof was ever sought.

> The 'scandal of philosophy' is not that this proof has yet to be given, but that such proofs are expected and attempted again and again. . . . It is not that the proofs are inadequate but that the kind of Being of the entity which does the proving and makes requests for proofs has not been made definite enough.[24]

The Cartesian thought experiment is only possible because thought and language are already in place. The possibility of thinking and speaking is bound up with a more fundamental way of encountering the world. The context of the world as an environment in which the human being finds itself is crucial for Heidegger's thought. The condition for all philosophy is a mode of existence as Being-in-the-world (*In-der-Welt-Sein*). It is this primordial setting that is overlooked in Descartes' thought, and consequently the picture of the bare subject looking out at the external world is thoroughly distorted.[25]

Descartes had organized everything in his ontology into two types of substance: mental and material (*res cogitans* and *res extensa*). Heidegger claims that this type of analysis is only possible because of a certain background or horizon of understanding. In the world which precedes and conditions human enquiry ideas of mind and matter are already grounded. There obtains a pre-reflective context of all human enquiry and it is the task of philosophy to enquire after this. Only when this is done can the question of Being be properly clarified. Heidegger approaches this question by examining the structures of human existence. It is in human existence that the question of Being is raised, and therefore by considering the being of humankind we can pursue the general question of Being. It is important to realize that Heidegger's exploration of human existence is directed towards this end, and that his analysis of human existence is therefore a preliminary task rather than the final goal of philosophical enquiry.

Human being is signified as *'Dasein'* by Heidegger. This means literally 'being there' or 'being here', and something incorporating both these senses is implied by the use of *'Dasein'*.[26] The being of *Dasein* must be distinguished from the being of things. It has been the mistake of theology and philosophy to define human beings as one amongst many types of thing in the world. This is to posit human beings as objects which can be classified alongside others. The possibility of such classification, however, presupposes a background of meaning and it is necessary to enquire into this pre-reflective setting. Only by attending to this prior horizon of meaning can philosophy make progress with the primordial question of Being.

> If its kind of Being as ready-to-hand is disregarded, this 'Nature' itself can be discovered and defined simply in its pure presence-at-hand. But when this happens, the Nature which 'stirs and strives', which assails us and enthralls us as landscape, remains hidden. The botanist's plants are not the flowers of the hedge-row; the 'source' which the geographer establishes for a river is not the 'springhead in the dale'.[27]

The being of *Dasein* is manifested in the phenomenon of care (*Sorge*). Care or concern is one of the fundamental features of *Dasein* and distinguishes human existence from the reality belonging to other entities. '*Dasein* is an entity for which, in its Being, that Being is an issue.'[28] In the phenomenon of care, other structures of human existence are brought to light. *Dasein* is fundamentally being-in-the-world. It is being which is situated in a world of things and other persons. *Dasein* belongs inextricably to a material and social world. The world is a place in which I find myself bound up in a network of relations with things and people. Material objects are known primarily as items of equipment which determine my practical concerns and other persons are those with whom I share the world. Here we have an analysis of human existence which is strikingly different from Descartes' picture of the isolated mental subject surveying a world which is known only indirectly through information supplied by the senses. The world is a complex set of relations in which I find myself, and it constitutes the pre-reflective context of all intellectual enquiry.

Heidegger writes of the 'thrownness' (*Geworfenheit*) of *Dasein*. The reality of the world does not have to be demonstrated for it is a presupposition of any demonstration. The human subject finds itself cast forth upon a world, and this facticity of existence must be reckoned with. Heidegger's analysis of existence then proceeds towards the notion of 'projection' (*Entwurf*). Human existence is not fixed and determinate; it contains potential and possibility. Here the relationship of being to time is crucial. Human existence is characterized by its temporality. It is existence oriented toward the future and, in particular, towards death (*Sein-zum-Tode*). Our thrownness towards death manifests itself above all in anxiety (*Angst*).[29] My death belongs peculiarly to me as my own possibility and, in the face of this, I can choose either to own it or to disown it. This creates a situation in which two basic possibilities emerge: one can live either authentically or inauthentically. Authentic (*eigentlich*) existence is attained when human beings own their existence, whereas inauthentic (*uneigentlich*) existence corresponds to the disowning of existence. This dual possibility of existence is central to Bultmann's appropriation of Heidegger.

For Heidegger, truth is not primarily a property belonging to propositions that accurately mirror external realities. Truth in its more ancient sense is the uncovering of what previously lies concealed. (The Greek word *alētheia* means literally 'unconcealment' or 'disclosure'.) It belongs to *Dasein* either to disclose or to conceal the truth. This disclosure occurs through an authentic understanding of the being that *Dasein* possesses. Truth is something that belongs to a mode of existence and only derivatively to propositions. Magda King writes:

> Whereas traditional philosophy has for long regarded the proposition as the primary locus of truth, Heidegger shows it to be a far-off derivative of original truth, whose 'locus' is the existential constitution of man's being as care.[30]

Heidegger's distinction between an existential (*existenzial*) analytic and an 'existentiell' (*existenziell*) understanding of *Dasein* is also important in this context.[31] The philosopher can produce an existential analysis of existence which delineates the formal structure of existence. An existentiell understanding however is the particular understanding of this existence which must be grasped by individuals in the actual situation of their lives. Understanding, as opposed to the intellectual apprehension of ideas, is the basic mode of existence. This understanding must be discovered personally and cannot be gained merely through grasping a philosophical analysis of existence. For Bultmann, as we shall see, this distinction is appealed to repeatedly in the face of criticism. His use of Heidegger's existential analytic does not preclude, he insists, a Christian existentiell understanding of human existence.

Understanding, for Heidegger, is a basic mode of existence rather than the intellectual grasp of ideas. Throughout the first division of *Being and Time*, Heidegger explores the ways in which we live inauthentically by disowning our existence. Humankind seeks to conceal its primordial existentiell condition by throwing itself into preoccupation with worldly things that lie at hand. The openness of existence makes it possible for us to fall (*verfallen*) away from owning our existence and from living authentically. In our average, everyday existence we are constantly concealing and evading our human condition. By absorbing ourselves in the familiar, everyday realities of our world we become a part of the world and therefore turn away from the most radical features of our existence such as our anxiety in the face of death.

> This evasive concealment in the face of death dominates everydayness so stubbornly that, in Being with one another, the 'neighbours' often still keep talking the 'dying person' into the belief that he will escape death and soon return to the tranquillized everydayness of the world of his concern . . . Indeed the dying of others is seen often enough as a social inconvenience, if not even a downright tactlessness, against which the public is to be guarded.[32]

By contrast, in owning our existence we find ourselves typically in the mood of dread (*Angst*). Dread is to be distinguished from fear. Fear always presupposes some definite threat, whereas the cause of dread is simply our human condition—its thrownness, its openness toward the future and its orientation towards death. Even in our pre-reflective experience we have a premonition of dread in our sense of the uncanny (*unheimlich*). Death is not merely the last event in a sequence, it is not something that is tacked on to the end of life; rather, the horizon set by death conditions the whole of life. *Dasein* is oriented towards death (*Sein-zum-Tode*) and this must be acknowledged in authentic existence. Thus the temporality of human existence is crucial to its condition. An authentic existentiell understanding is one in which I acknowledge my condition and shoulder personal responsibility for my own existence. This act of owning my existence is marked by resoluteness (*Entschlossenheit*).

Heidegger believed that the analysis of human existence presented in *Being and Time* would provide a pathway to the more fundamental question of Being. In uncovering the hidden possibilities of thought and language he hoped to find a way to the forgotten question of Being. It is clear however that the end of his philosophical enquiry was not reached in this book, and the fact that the projected third division on 'Time' was never completed perhaps indicates that he believed it could not be reached in this way. In his later philosophy, which some critics argue represents a turn in his thought, there is less analysis of individual human existence and more attention to the general question of Being through the exploration of language. However, a discussion of Heidegger's later philosophy is not necessary for the purposes of examining his influence upon Bultmann. It is the Heidegger of the 1920s, and especially of *Being and Time*, who remains decisive for Bultmann. We can now examine his use of this philosophy.

The appropriation of Heidegger

In the history of theology we can detect a variety of attitudes towards philosophy. Some theologians have held to the view that the truths of the Christian faith are continuous with and an extension of the religious truths that are accessible to the philosopher. This conception of an essential harmony and continuity can be found in Justin Martyr in the second century and Karl Jaspers in the twentieth. On the other hand, there have been those who have regarded philosophy with considerable suspicion and have seen it as threatening to subvert the truth to which Christian faith alone can witness. We could mention, in this context, Tertullian at the beginning of the third century and Karl Barth in the twentieth. Bultmann stands somewhere between these two positions.

We have already spoken of Bultmann's belief in the importance of philosophy for the task of the existential interpretation of Scripture. Theologians require a set of concepts which will enable them to express the Christian understanding of existence. In order to do this, language about what it means to be human will inevitably be employed, and here the theologian is ineluctably committed to borrowing from the philosopher. While theology has its own subject matter—the word of God—of which philosophy knows nothing, the theologian is committed, nonetheless, to using philosophical concepts in expressing the understanding of existence made possible by God's word. Here the philosopher and the theologian share what John Macquarrie calls 'zones of common interest'.[33]

We must also bear in mind the extent to which Bultmann's search for an appropriate conceptuality was determined by his indebtedness to the theology of Wilhelm Herrmann. Following Herrmann, Bultmann insists that theology cannot be assimilated to a worldview, a metaphysic or a dogmatic system. Christian faith as a personal and particular relationship with God is distorted if it is translated into an 'objective' idiom. The language of theology must preserve the inward and existential character of faith. To a large degree, it is this theological conviction, derived mainly from Herrmann, that disposes Bultmann towards the philosophy of Heidegger. Significantly, he could write to Barth in a letter of November 1952: 'It was because I learned from Herrmann, that I was ready for Heidegger'.[34]

Heidegger's philosophy was in many ways another catalyst that Bultmann was waiting for, and their collaboration in Marburg during the 1920s left a permanent mark on all of Bultmann's theological writings. Due to the unavailability of the language of metaphysics and dogmatics, Bultmann finds in Heidegger's existential analytic the most suitable conceptuality for doing theology, i.e. for articulating the Christian understanding of existence.

> I found in it the conceptuality in which it is possible to speak adequately of human existence and therefore also of the existence of the believer.[35]

The following themes in Heidegger's philosophy figure prominently in Bultmann, and throughout the 1920s we can see them featuring in his theological and exegetical essays.[36]
1. The emphasis upon the preunderstanding is in part something that both Bultmann and Heidegger inherit from their common intellectual heritage, yet there is no doubt that the prominence of the

Vorverständnis in Heidegger largely explains its appearance in Bultmann. For Heidegger, there is in human existence a pre-reflective awareness of Being and it is the task of philosophy to uncover this. This preunderstanding is not so much intellectual as existential. It belongs to a mode of existence rather than to a purely cerebral process. Similarly, in Bultmann's use of the preunderstanding the question of God is alive not as a cosmological hypothesis but in the enquiry about the deepest issues confronting individuals.

2. Bultmann's emphasis upon the historicity of *Dasein* is heavily influenced by Heidegger. The human being lives in time and is confronted with fundamental choices about how to live and how to face the future. There are, in Heidegger, two basic possibilities of existence—authentic and inauthentic existence. These are axiomatic to Bultmann's theological interpretation and enable him to view human life in terms of two theological possibilities; existence prior to faith and existence under faith. This emerges most clearly in his interpretation of Paul and the doctrine of justification.

3. Heidegger's distinction between 'existential' and 'existentiell' is also embedded in Bultmann's thought. Existential analysis is an ontological description of certain formal features of human life. While this is borrowed from Heidegger, the theologian remains free to say what constitutes an existentiell understanding on the basis of actual ontic reality. There is a sense in which the conceptual containers provided by Heidegger's philosophy are to be filled with Christian existentiell content.

> The claim of faith that there is only *one* word that has this power is not discussible for ontological analysis, and the assertion that this word is the word of God is for it absurd, for it knows only man and nothing beyond him. On the other hand, however, the claim of faith that the word of proclamation is the word of God and therefore is spoken to man from the beyond does not at all mean that this word does not at the same time encounter us as a phenomenon of human existence. That it is the word of God is not to be seen, but only to be believed; and to be able to show what this means, what is meant therefore by 'the word became flesh', is precisely an indirect result of existential analysis.[37]

As we have already noted, a common criticism of Bultmann is that he has sold out to a fashionable philosophy. Christian theology, it is claimed, has been collapsed into existentialism. The situation however is not as simple as this. Bultmann and Heidegger themselves both disclaimed the view that the former's theology had been constructed upon the latter's philosophy,[38] and the charge of mere assimilation can be countered in at least four ways.

Firstly, Bultmann's theological agenda was largely established prior to the influence of Heidegger. His basic orientation is already determined with the influence of Herrmann and, therefore, Heidegger is appropriated for a pre-conceived purpose. We have already seen the extent to which Bultmann's theology took shape prior to his 1922 encounter with Heidegger.

Secondly, the distinction between the existential and the existentiell is designed to safeguard the autonomy of revelation. There is no sense in which the philosophical preunderstanding contains an implicit faith or a pre-reflective knowledge of revelation.[39] Heidegger's analytic is merely used as a formal conceptuality for the theological task. His philosophy is not a metaphysical system which controls what the theologian can or cannot say. It simply provides the theologian with an appropriate set of categories for reflecting upon human existence.

> If one understands philosophy as the critical science of being (*Sein*)—that is, as the science which must control all the positive sciences dealing with beings (*Seienden*)—then philosophy does indeed do theology an indispensable service.[40]

Thirdly, as Bultmann constantly insisted in debate with Barth, the theologian cannot avoid using the most appropriate philosophical analysis of human existence that is available, in order to execute the tasks of theology. The history of Christian thought shows the manner in which every theology requires a set of ontological concepts with which to work. If this is not done critically theology will become imprisoned by an outmoded ontology. This is not to say that Heidegger's analysis is eternally valid, only that it is the best currently on offer. 'There is no alternative, it (philosophy) must be either maid or mistress.'[41]

Finally, Bultmann has defended the propriety of Heidegger's philosophy by pointing to the determinative influence of biblical thought patterns upon it. Heidegger's own work, and existentialism generally, have been affected by Christian thinkers from Paul to Kierkegaard. It is therefore not possible to dismiss Heidegger's philosophy as alien to the Christian faith. It itself retains an implicitly theological character.[42]

In these different ways, Bultmann is able to defend himself against the charge that he has capitulated to the most fashionable philosophy of the day. Nonetheless, his appropriation of Heidegger's work is not without difficulties. It is possible to accept that the theologian is committed to employing philosophical concepts while continuing to ask whether Heidegger's are the most appropriate. Heidegger's intention throughout his philosophy is to enquire into the nature of Being. The existential analysis in *Being and Time* is designed to serve this purpose. The distinction between 'existential' and 'existentiell' is made with the question of Being in mind, and the insistence upon the pre-reflective understanding is made with reference to Being itself and not to God. Heidegger is not in the business of providing a neutral analysis of existence which can be appropriated by a thinker with another purpose. His categories all contribute to the uncovering of the nature of Being, and it is not clear that a theologian wishing to expound the Christian faith can adopt Heideggerian themes, without distorting both Heidegger and the subject matter of theology.[43]

A further problem can be discerned in the ambivalent notion of the preunderstanding. According to Bultmann, interpreters can bring the most fundamental questions of human existence to the text. They can do this in virtue of the preunderstanding available to them as human beings, and through this preunderstanding it is possible for the word of God to be heard and received. At this point however Bultmann becomes hazy. In order that the word of God may connect with the preunderstanding, it is necessary to present that preunderstanding in a theological light. There must be a point of contact between natural human understanding and the word of God.[44] Bultmann recognizes this by insisting that the question of God is alive in the deepest questions of human existence. The interpreter who brings the question of God to the text will be able to hear the answer that is being proclaimed. Thus in describing the hermeneutical preunderstanding, human existence must be presented in a theological light. But this preunderstanding is also reckoned to be accessible to the philosopher; the word of God has not yet been spoken of and thinkers who analyse their existence can presumably formulate this preunderstanding. The problem is that this preunderstanding requires a theological character for Bultmann, but, according to his hermeneutical theory, it can be presented independently of any specific theological claim. For the preunderstanding to do the work that Bultmann requires of it, he must place a theological construction upon it. Yet it is not clear that he has a warrant to do this in terms of his existential analysis. The philosopher Gadamer has pointed to this difficulty in Bultmann's hermeneutical theory:

> The presupposition that one is moved by the question of God already involves a claim to knowledge concerning the true God and his revelation. Even unbelief is defined in terms of the faith that is demanded of one. The existential fore-understanding, which is Bultmann's starting point, can only be a christian one.[45]

Bultmann's best response to this difficulty would be to concede that the preunderstanding can only be theologically identified from the standpoint of faith. His description of human existence prior to faith would thus be a retrospective one. We only know that human existence enquires after God with the benefit of Christian hindsight. In doing this however the preunderstanding would be clearly brought under the control of positive theology, and the role of existential philosophy would subsequently diminish. Thus to salvage his analysis, Bultmann needs to assign a more subordinate role (though not an insignificant one) to philosophy than his position can concede.

An even more important question that arises is whether Bultmann's use of Heideggerian categories enables the theologian to present a true and adequate interpretation of the New Testament. This is the litmus test for his hermeneutical theory. There is certainly no doubt that Bultmann's deployment of existentialist categories not only affects a preliminary sketch of human existence, but also has a profound bearing upon the way the Christian faith is described. Heidegger's dual possibilities of inauthentic and authentic existence are transposed, in Bultmann's theology, into existence prior to faith and existence under faith. Therefore, we must turn to his theology of the New Testament to assess more fully the results of his appropriation of Heidegger.

Notes

1   F. Schleiermacher, *Hermeneutics: The Handwritten Manuscripts*, ed. H. Kimmerle (Missoula, MT, 1977). For an important discussion of the hermeneutical circle see H.G. Gadamer, *Truth and Method* (London, 1975), pp. 235–344.

2   Richard Palmer, *Hermeneutics* (Northwestern University Press, Evanston, 1969) pp. 88–90.

3   From selected passages of Dilthey's work in H. A. Hodges, *Wilhelm Dilthey* (Routledge and Kegan Paul, London, 1969), p. 142.

4   Cf. Palmer, p. 101.

5   This is developed most clearly in 'Das Problem der Hermeneutik' (1950); 'The problem of hermeneutics', NTM, pp. 72–3.

6   'Ist voraussetzungslose Exegese möglich?' (1957): 'Is exegesis without pressuppositions possible?', EF, p. 347.

7   'The problem of hermeneutics', p. 83.

8   Ibid.

9   'Is exegesis without presuppositions possible?', p. 151.

10 'The problem of hermeneutics', p. 86.

11 Ibid., p. 87.

12 Ibid., p. 84.

13 'Das Problem einer theologischen Exegese des Neuen Testaments' (1925); 'The problem of a theological exegesis of the New Testament' in James Robinson (ed.), *The Beginnings of Dialectical Theology* (Richmond, 1968), p. 241. The translation of *Sachexegese* and *Sachkritik* as 'objective exegesis' and 'objective criticism' is somewhat misleading as the important term *objectivieren* and its cognates are generally used by Bultmann in another sense.

14 Bultmann draws this comparison with Luther in TNT II, p. 238. For a discussion of Bultmann's method of *Sachkritik* see Robert Morgan, *The Nature of New Testament Theology* (SCM, London, 1973), pp. 42ff.

15 Cf. Terry Eagleton, *Literary Theory* (Blackwell, Oxford, 1983), ch. 4.

16 For a discussion of Bultmann's use of this distinction see John Painter, *Theology As Hermeneutics* (Sheffield, 1987), pp. 76–89.

17 Karl Barth, *The Epistle to the Romans*, trans. E. Hoskyns (Oxford, 1933), p. 7.

18 'Karl Barths Römerbrief in zweiter Auflage'; 'Review of Barth's Romans', *The Beginnings of Dialectical Theology*, pp. 100–20.

19 'Is exegesis without presuppositions possible?', pp. 146–51.

20 'Theologie als Wissenschaft' (1941); 'Theology as science', NTM, p. 63. Cf. TE, p. 35–65.

21 TNT II, pp. 240ff.

22 Cf. *Letters*, p. 76; W. Schmithals, *An Introduction to the Theology of Rudolf Bultmann* (London, 1968), ch. 1.

23 Bultmann wrote in the second edition of GV I (1954) 'This book

remains dedicated to Martin Heidegger in grateful memory of our time together in Marburg'.

24 *Being and Time*, trans. J. Macquarrie and E. Robinson (Blackwell, Oxford, 1962), p. 249.

25 For a study of the anti-Cartesian nature of Heidegger's philosophy see Charles Guignon, *Heidegger and the Problem of Knowledge* (Indianapolis, 1983). A similar critique of Descartes can be discerned in the writings of Wittgenstein, e.g. *Philosophical Investigations* (trans. G.E. Anscombe; Blackwell, Oxford, 1958). This aspect of Wittgenstein's thought is discussed from a theological perspective by Fergus Kerr, *Theology After Wittgenstein* (Blackwell, Oxford, 1987).

26 Cf. Magda King, *Heidegger's Philosophy: A Guide to His Basic Thought* (Blackwell, Oxford, 1964), p. 67.

27 *Being and Time*, p. 100.

28 Ibid., p. 236.

29 Ibid., sections 50–1.

30 Magda King, p. 141.

31 *Being and Time*, section 4.

32 Ibid., pp. 297–8.

33 'Philosophy and theology in Bultmann's thought' in C.W. Kegley (ed.), *The Theology of Rudolf Bultmann* (SCM, London, 1966), p. 130. Macquarrie's *An Existentialist Theology* (London, 1955) remains a most helpful guide to the relationship between Bultmann and Heidegger.

34 *Letters*, p. 99. This connection between the influence of Herrmann and Heidegger is noted by Michael Beintker, *Die Gottesfrage in der Theologie Wilhelm Herrmanns* (Berlin, 1976), p. 126. Cf. the discussion of the connections between Herrmann, Barth and Bultmann in Jürgen Moltmann, *Theology of Hope* (London, 1967), pp. 50ff.; and J.C. O'Neill, 'Bultmann and Hegel', *Journal of Theological Studies* 21 (1970), pp. 391ff.

35 'Autobiographical reflections', EF, p. 341. Bultmann described Heidegger's *Being and Time* as one of the six most influential books in his thought: 'Milestones in books', *Expository Times* LXX (1958/59), p. 125.

36 Cf. the essays collected in GV I and trans. in FU. In 1929 Gerhard Kuhlmann wrote an essay criticizing Bultmann's extensive use of Heidegger: 'Zum theologischen Problem der Existenz: Fragen an Rudolf Bultmann', *Zeitschrift für Theologie und Kirche* (1929), pp. 28–57. Bultmann responded to this in the essay 'Die Geschichtlichkeit des Daseins und der Glaube'; 'The historicity of man (*Dasein*) and faith', EF, pp. 107–29.

37 'The historicity of man and faith', p. 129.

38 G.W. Ittel cites letters written by Heidegger and Bultmann in 1954 which make this disclaimer: 'Der Einfluss der Philosophie M. Heideggers auf die Theologie R. Bultmanns' in *Kerygma und Dogma* (1956), p. 91.

39 Cf. 'Anknüpfung und Widerspruch' (1946); 'Points of contact and conflict ', EPT, pp. 133–51.

40 'Vom Begriff der religiösen Gemeinschaft', *Theologische Blätter* VI (1927), col. 73. The translation is my own.

41 *Letters*, p. 39.

42 Ibid., p. 98.

43 Bultmann has often been charged with misreading Heidegger by treating his *Daseinsanalytik* as an anthropology: e.g. Heinrich Ott, *Geschichte und Heilsgeschichte in der Theologie Rudolf Bultmanns* (Tübingen, 1955), p. 173; Eberhard Jüngel, *Glauben und Verstehen* (Heidelberg, 1985), p. 20. For a defence of his use of Heidegger see A. Malet, *The Thought of Rudolf Bultmann* (Shannon, 1969), pp. 298–336.

44 Cf. 'Points of contact and conflict', pp. 135–8.

45 H.G. Gadamer, *Truth and Method*, p. 296. Gareth Jones has recently made the interesting suggestion that Bultmann should be seen as 'a positive philosopher of the Christian religion' whose work in certain respects is much closer to Kierkegaard than to Heidegger: *Bultmann: Towards a Critical Theology* (Oxford, 1991), p. 78.

5

The Theology of the New Testament

I. JESUS

The most common perception of Bultmann amongst students of theology is of a New Testament critic who is radically sceptical about the extent of our knowledge of the historical Jesus. On this view, Bultmann is a dangerous maverick whose work threatens to undermine the foundations of the Christian faith. Although this perception is mistaken it is not difficult to see how it has arisen from some of Bultmann's more provocative statements.

> I do indeed think that we can know almost nothing concerning the life and personality of Jesus, since the early Christian sources show no interest in either, are moreover fragmentary and often legendary; and other sources about Jesus do not exist. (*Jesus*, p. 8)

A statement such as the above can easily create the impression that Bultmann's critical work is primarily destructive of Christian faith. We must recognize, however, that there are both historical and theological constraints upon his scepticism. As an historian, Bultmann considers that, while the gospels do not furnish us with a biography of the life of Jesus or a description of his personality, they do nonetheless tell us much about the things he said and did. In this sense, we can uncover a good deal of authentic information about the historical Jesus. As a theologian, moreover, Bultmann believes that this limitation upon historical knowledge is to be welcomed rather than deplored. The proclamation of the New Testament concerns the death and resurrection of Jesus. The Christian kerygma deals with the 'that' of the cross rather than the 'what' and the 'how' of the circumstances preceding it. The quest of the historical Jesus is not essential to Christian preaching, for it is not the Church's task to probe into the psyche of Jesus, but only to proclaim him as the Saviour through his death and resurrection.

Despite the theological focus of the New Testament upon the crucifixion of Jesus, it is possible for the historian to study the gospels in an attempt to understand the circumstances of his life. These circumstances precede the rise of the Christian faith and enable us better to understand it. The historical work that was pursued, mainly in Germany, during the nineteenth and early twentieth centuries was concerned with reconstructing the life of the historical Jesus from the sources available to us. While Wrede, Schweitzer and others had drawn attention to the difficulties and limitations of this task, it had never been abandoned. Bultmann remains within this tradition of attempting to discover the historical Jesus through the methods of scientific history.

The synoptic tradition

At the beginning of the twentieth century something approaching a consensus had emerged amongst critics of the gospel tradition. It was assumed that the Marcan hypothesis was, broadly speaking, correct. According to this theory, the synoptic gospels were based upon two primary sources; Mark and Q, a collection of sayings of Jesus sometimes referred to by Bultmann as the Logia. The fourth gospel, representing a later and more distinct tradition, was generally not regarded as an important source for reconstructing Jesus' words and actions. Consequently, any reconstruction of the life of Jesus had to be based principally upon an analysis of Mark and Q.

In *The History of the Synoptic Tradition*[1] Bultmann broke new ground in the quest for the historical Jesus with his use of the methods of form criticism. Following the work of Wrede and Wellhausen, he assumed that Mark's gospel did not furnish us with an outline of the development of the ministry of Jesus. He argued, instead, that Mark had used a source, comprising a disconnected series of individual units (pericopae) which recounted incidents or sayings in the life of Jesus. The arguments upon which this position was erected had already been mapped out by Wrede. These referred to the absence of any messianic consciousness in Jesus; the organization of

Mark's material around theological and apologetical, rather than historical criteria; and the way in which much of the material in Mark could only be explained by its use in the early Church as opposed to the life of Jesus. In the light of these arguments, it was claimed that the individual units had been elaborated or even created for the purposes of the life and mission of the early Christian communities. As historical sources, they provide us primarily with information about the early Church, and only secondarily with information about the preceding life of Jesus.

The analysis of the history of forms (*Formgeschichte*) was pioneered by the Old Testament scholar Hermann Gunkel, in his work on the psalms. It was claimed that the component parts were formed by the creation and transmission of oral tradition which subsequently appeared as literary tradition.[2] By establishing the laws which govern the forming of such tradition and its setting in the life of a historical community, Gunkel tried to discern the ways in which individual units had developed. On the basis of this, it was possible to speculate, with varying degrees of probability, as to the original content of these units.

In the case of the synoptic tradition, Dibelius, Bultmann and others argued that we can discover the rules which govern the formation of tradition by examining contemporary rabbinical literature and the apocryphal gospels. In addition, we have valuable clues to the manner in which the Christian tradition was formed through examining the ways in which Matthew and Luke adapted their main source, Mark. There are, however, difficulties which the form critic faces when analysing Mark. There is the obvious one that we do not have access to Mark's sources and, therefore, cannot be certain as to how much he has adapted these. Moreover, unlike the development of much of the Old Testament, the gospels are the products of a relatively brief tradition. Mark was probably written within forty years of the events narrated in the gospel.[3]

In his analysis of the synoptic tradition, Bultmann classifies the different units into four categories (although within and across these categories there are further sub-divisions). We can examine each of these briefly.[4]

(a) *Apophthegms*. These are short passages in the gospels which seek to present a saying of Jesus or an incident which depicts his character. The significant thing at the heart of each of these is the utterance or the quality of character illustrated. The narrative material tends to be brief and is occasionally embellished in order to highlight the saying or the action of Jesus. This literary type is apparent in rabbinical writings which provide illuminating comparative material. One species of apophthegm concerns those utterances which provide Jesus' response to a particular controversy. For example, in Mark 3:1–6, the controversy over the observance of the Sabbath is resolved by Jesus asking a question of his opponents. 'Is it lawful on the sabbath to do good or to do harm, to save life or to kill?' This saying is to be understood primarily in terms of its relevance to disputes encountered within the early Church. Its *Sitz im Leben* (life setting) is, therefore, to be located in the life of the Church rather than the life of the historical Jesus. Bultmann is ready, on occasion, to concede that the dispute over the observance of the sabbath may have occurred in the life of Jesus and that he may have spoken in terms similar to Mark 3:4. But we can only be led to this conclusion when first we have discovered the ecclesial context of the pericope (HST, p. 40).

The biographical apophthegms tend to highlight some aspect of Jesus' character or ministry rather than displaying an interest in historical or psychological explanation. A clear example of this is the calling of the disciples in Mark 1:16–20 and 2:14. The point of these stories is to show how Jesus summons men and women from the everyday business of life, demanding total allegiance of them. Doubtless, there were disciples who did abandon their previous forms of life to follow Jesus, but the point of these pericopae is not primarily to furnish the reader with this historical information. The point is to illustrate the summons of Jesus (ibid., p. 28).

(b) *Dominical sayings*. The sayings of Jesus in Mark and Q can be gathered together into different categories which display various thematic similarities. The most important types of saying are the wisdom utterances, the precepts or legal sayings, and the prophetic and apocalyptic utterances. Much of the material generally attributed to the Q source belongs to the first category of wisdom sayings, e.g. the passage in the Sermon on the Mount about unnecessary anxiety (Matt 6:25–34). Many of these sayings have direct parallels in rabbinic literature, and it is possible that these words may have either been quoted by Jesus or put into his mouth by a Christian scribe, familiar with the rabbinic sources. In the light of this, Bultmann does not consider these wisdom sayings a reliable guide to the actual words of Jesus (HST, pp. 101ff.).

However, he is more confident that some of the precepts or legal sayings have their origin in Jesus' ministry. As it is not possible that all these sayings could have been either taken over from Judaism or invented by the early Church, we must assume that they come from Jesus himself. This is essentially a use of the criterion of dissimilarity. By identifying what cannot have been invented by the Church or borrowed from contemporary culture we isolate bedrock material which can only come from the historical Jesus. Material that is thus rendered dissimilar is assumed to be authentic. By arguing that certain sayings can only have a *Sitz im Leben* in the life of Jesus rather than the life of the early Church, Bultmann is able to establish genuine information about the former. Whereas Matthew 5:17–19 is to be explained by debates about the Law being conducted in the early Christian community, Matthew 5:21–48 must reflect, at least in part, Jesus' controversy with traditional Jewish piety (ibid., p. 147).

The prophetic and apocalyptic sayings are those in which Jesus proclaims the coming of the kingdom of God, and, here also, Bultmann believes that we receive distinct echoes of the authentic words of Jesus. Some of the apocalyptic passages in the gospels certainly appear to be the adaptation by the Christian community of traditional Jewish images. This can be seen by the way in which their *Sitz im Leben* reflects the situation of the early Church and not that of the historical Jesus. The attempt to provide an adequate response to the problem of the delay of the Parousia is reflected for instance in Matthew 24:10–12 (HST, p. 126). Yet it is highly probable that Jesus appeared as an eschatological prophet who announced the kingdom of God, and that his message was one of grace and of judgement. In support of this, Bultmann argues that many of the eschatological sayings in the gospels can only be attributed to Jesus rather than to the Church or Judaism. In the Beatitudes, for example, we find an 'acute eschatological consciousness with its combined gladness and gravity in the face of decision'. The distinctive nature of this eschatological consciousness strongly suggests that it comes only from Jesus (ibid., p. 128).

(c) *Miracle stories*. Bultmann's confidence that many of the sayings have their origin in the words of the historical Jesus tends to diminish when he comes to examine the narrative material in the gospels. In the case of the miracle stories, this scepticism is largely based on the fact that they belong to a literary type common in Hellenistic literature (HST, pp. 220ff.). This typical pattern involves, in the case of healing miracles: a description of the nature of the illness; an account of the details of the healing; and finally a report about the effect of the miracle on the onlookers in terms of astonishment, approval or terror. It is common, moreover, in the ancient world, for tales of miracles to grow around the memory of heroes and leaders. Sometimes these stories originate in connection with some saying of the celebrated individual. Bultmann tends to conclude that the miracle stories have evolved in this way, and that their particular details reflect the interests of the early Christian community. While healings and exorcisms may well have marked the ministry of Jesus (*Jesus*, p. 73), the accounts we have of these conform to traditional patterns and are couched in legendary terms.

(d) *Historical stories and legends.* Bultmann argues that many of the key events narrated by the synoptic writers are legendary in quality. It is this claim more than any other which makes it impossible to construct a biography of Jesus. A legend is defined in the following way:

> I would describe legends as those parts of the tradition which are not miracle stories in the proper sense, but instead of being historical in character are religious and edifying. (HST, p. 244)

Many of the key events in the gospel narratives are classified as legends. The baptism of Jesus by John (while itself rooted in history) is described in a way that is legendary, particularly in terms of its consecration of Jesus as Messiah (HST, pp. 247ff.). Peter's confession at Caesarea Philippi (Mark 8:27–30) is a literary device designed to highlight the distinctive faith of the early Church (HST, p. 258). The triumphal entry into Jerusalem 'became a Messianic legend under the influence of Zechariah 9:9' (ibid., p. 262). The Last Supper has been edited into an account of a Passover meal with reference to the sacrificial death of Jesus (ibid., p. 266). In the resurrection narratives, the empty tomb stories are apologetic legends while the appearance stories have the functions of proving the resurrection and legitimizing the missionary task of the Church (ibid., pp. 284ff.).

It is not possible to do justice here to Bultmann's careful arguments for these conclusions regarding the legendary status of the narrative material. Their cumulative force, however, is to demonstrate that Jesus did not speak or act as the Messiah. Most of the events in the gospels which provide the basis for a theology of the person of Christ are undermined by Bultmann's classification of them as legendary. The possibility of the gospel narratives disclosing the identity of Jesus through his life and ministry is removed by Bultmann's claim that the crucial events recounted there are not the causes of faith in Jesus, so much as the effects of faith. The Christian faith does not emerge through an appreciation of Jesus' life and ministry; it emerges only through the impact of his death and resurrection. The accounts that we now have of his life have been preserved, amended and edited in order to proclaim this faith.

The historical Jesus

We have begun to see the extent of Bultmann's historical scepticism. Its upshot is twofold. It is claimed both that the knowledge we have of the historical Jesus tends to be confined to his characteristic utterances, and that these do not belong to the essence of the Christian faith. It is this twofold conclusion which explains why the message of the historical Jesus is dealt with in a brief introduction to the two-volume *Theology of the New Testament*.

The message of Jesus is a presupposition for the theology of the New Testament rather than a part of that theology itself. (TNT I, p. 3)

Despite this assessment, Bultmann presents, in *Jesus and the Word*, a powerful description of the teaching of the historical Jesus. This book reveals the more positive results of form criticism and offers us an account of Jesus' message as the harbinger of the post-Easter understanding of existence.

Little as we know of his life and personality, we know enough of his *message* to make for ourselves a consistent picture. (*Jesus*, p. 12)

The message of Jesus is rooted in the soil of Jewish eschatology. The kingdom of God is proclaimed as imminent and it is described in apocalyptic terms. The Son of Man will appear as God's emissary. The dead will rise, and under God's judgement they will inherit the glory of heaven or the damnation of hell. The force of this message is not to encourage speculation about the future, but to confront men and women with the urgency of decision in the present time. God's future determines the present. A decision now will determine one's ultimate destiny.

If men are standing in the crisis of decision, and if precisely this crisis is the essential characteristic of their humanity, then every hour is the last hour. (*Jesus*, p. 52)

This message is further conditioned by Jesus' teaching as a Jewish rabbi, for he appears both as an eschatological prophet and as a teacher of the law. Jesus asserted the traditional authority of the law but, at the same time, radicalized the idea of obedience to the law. He does this, for example, in the antitheses of the Sermon on the Mount, by setting one passage of Scripture over against another. (In this respect, Jesus was an early exponent of *Sachkritik*!) Radical obedience involves not only outward conformity to the law, but the determination of one's whole being by the essential demands of that law (*Jesus*, p. 77).

Under the radical demands of God all human living is exposed as sinful; the only hope is to abandon oneself to divine forgiveness and grace. In Jesus' message, we see both the total demand and the total grace of God. In the parable of the tax-collector and the Pharisee (Luke 18:9–14), and the endorsement of the poor and children, we discover the only attitude that is appropriate before the judgement and mercy of God. In this proclamation, we encounter 'the remote and the near God'. God is not to be apprehended in terms of general truths and dogmas, but only through an encounter with the word of Jesus which calls forth decision and commitment (*Jesus*, p. 151). (There is no doubt that here Bultmann is using the message of the historical Jesus to articulate his own theological interests. In this respect, *Jesus and the Word* is an essay in dialectical theology. It is curious that the message of the historical Jesus is used as a vehicle for Bultmann's theology, given his insistence elsewhere that it is a presupposition of Christian faith rather than a part of that faith.)

While the teaching of Jesus concerns the message of the kingdom, the later proclamation of the Church has not the kingdom but Jesus at its centre. In this respect, Jesus displaces the kingdom in the kerygma. It is the message of Christ crucified that represents God's act of deliverance for the sinner and not the words of Jesus. Again, we see Bultmann's historical conclusions meshing with his theological assumptions.

Presuppositions of form criticism

Before proceeding to examine his interpretation of Paul and John we should pause to consider some possible lines of criticism of

Bultmann's treatment of the synoptic gospels. This is a necessary task for anyone who wishes to challenge his theological conclusions.

In assessing form criticism, it is first necessary to realize that, as a method of investigation, it is an essential tool. We know from the witness of Papias ('I supposed that things out of books did not profit me so much as the utterances of a voice which lives and abides'[5]) that there existed an oral tradition within the Church both alongside and prior to the written records that we now possess. This tradition, presumably, comprised a series of quasi-independent units which could be recounted as occasion demanded. When we read the opening chapters of Mark we are struck by the manner in which a series of incidents is narrated which appear to be disconnected. The ordering of the series appears to be topical rather than chronological as the different arrangements in Matthew and Luke confirm.[6] Given this setting of the synoptic material, it is entirely proper to investigate the manner in which these units have been formed and have come to expression in the written gospels. However, there remain problems relating to the determination of the material by the specific concerns of the early Christian community.

In form criticism, there is a hermeneutical circularity involved in the explanation of the material by the *Sitze im Leben* of the early Church. Our knowledge of the early Church is derived, in part, from the synoptic material (although the Acts and the Epistles can function as an independent check), and yet that same material is to be explained by the knowledge it yields.[7] While this circularity is unavoidable in historical enquiry, it creates certain dangers. If the form critic is preoccupied with using the sources to establish a picture of the early community, then the subsequent explanation of that material may overestimate the creative forces at work in the community, while underestimating the interest in the historical Jesus. Consequently, the conservative dimension of the tradition will be underplayed. An insistent appeal to the life-setting of the community as the explanation for the material may obscure the roots of the kerygma in the ministry of Jesus. The method is capable of distorting as well as illuminating the nature of the material.

It is clear, moreover, that form criticism works better for some aspects of the material than for others. In the case of the parables, the controversial utterances and the miracle stories, we can discern something like a recognizable literary or oral type. In each case, there is a distinctive pattern and shape to the pericope which make form-critical analysis fruitful. But in the case of the narrative material which Bultmann assigns to the status of 'legend', it is not so clear that we are dealing with a distinctive type. There is no apparent parallel with the distinctive pattern of many of the miracle stories.[8] Alongside this criticism, there is a perceived need to ask how the narrative material originated and what was the interest of the community in preserving it.[9] Unlike other Jewish communities, the early Christians were not merely interested in preserving the sayings of Jesus. For the Church, Jesus was more than a rabbi and this is reflected in the way in which narrative material is transmitted. In particular, we have to reckon with the shape of the Passion story, which appears as much less disconnected than the earlier parts of Mark.

A further methodological issue concerns the use of the dissimilarity criterion to establish information about the historical Jesus. While this criterion is undoubtedly useful in establishing 'a critically assured minimum', it cannot be the sole criterion for our information about the historical Jesus. By excluding any clear parallel with contemporary Judaism or the interests of the Church, this criterion, if used exclusively, outlaws any possible continuity between Jesus and the Church.[10] In order to make sense of the origins of Christianity, we need to have recourse to wider criteria such as multiple attestation, the unintentional yielding of data, and coherence. Only thus can we hope to establish a more complete picture of the words and actions of Jesus.[11]

This questioning of the methods of Bultmann's form criticism should suggest neither that historical critical study is to be abandoned nor that the gospels are merely faithful transmissions of the original witnesses. (The extent to which Matthew and Luke have edited Mark clearly shows this.) It does suggest, however, that the execution of form criticism may lead to a relative neglect of certain features of the synoptic tradition and, consequently, to conclusions about the historical Jesus which are unnecessarily sceptical. We shall return to this vexed subject in the closing chapter.

II. PAUL

Although the words of Jesus are transmitted by the synoptic tradition, it is clear that, for the early Church, it is not so much the message as its bearer who is proclaimed. The Christian kerygma has at its centre not Jesus' teaching about the kingdom of God but Jesus himself as the crucified Christ. Jesus is proclaimed as the eschatological Messiah rather than as a teacher or as a prophet. 'The proclaimer became the proclaimed' (TNT I, p. 33). For the early Church, Jesus is, first and foremost, the Messiah who is expected to return as God's emissary to judge the world. This is apparent from the manner in which the Church lives as an 'eschatological congregation' (ibid., pp. 37–42).

The watershed between the proclamation of Jesus and that of the Church was the crucifixion. For the Jewish mind, crucifixion was a scandalous curse and, therefore, a radically new understanding had to emerge for the crucified Jesus to be acknowledged as the Messiah. Bultmann has surprisingly little to say about the historical causes of this new understanding, and he certainly does not want to appeal to either the empty tomb or the resurrection appearances. As we shall see in the subsequent chapter, his theology of the resurrection prevents this move being made.

> How this act of decision took place in detail, how the Easter faith arose in individual disciples, has been obscured in the tradition by legend and is not of basic importance. . . . The accounts of the empty grave, of which Paul still knows nothing, are legends. According to 1 Cor. 15.5–8, where Paul enumerates the appearances of the risen Lord as tradition offered them, the resurrection of Jesus meant simultaneously his exaltation; not until later was the resurrection interpreted as a temporary return to life on earth, and this idea then gave rise to the ascension story. (TNT I, p. 45)

In the writings of Paul, we encounter Christianity in a Hellenistic setting. Paul does not stand in the tradition of preserving a record of the words and deeds of Jesus and he does not refer to him as the apocalyptic Son of Man. While continuing to look forward to the imminent return of Jesus at the close of the age, Paul's thinking is less dominated by this conception than is the synoptic tradition. For Paul, theology and anthropology are inextricably connected. Everything he says about God is in relation to God's determination of the human situation, and everything he says about human beings is governed by what can be said about God. In the light of this, Bultmann considers it appropriate to organize Pauline theology under the two divisions 'existence prior to the revelation of faith' and 'existence under faith'.

Existence prior to faith

Bultmann gives an account of Paul's understanding of human existence prior to faith by considering his leading anthropological terms.
Here the crucial concept is that of *sōma*, body. According to
Bultmann, Paul's main use of this term is not to refer to the physical
body of a human being but to one's total way of relating to self,
world and God. The manner in which *sōma* can denote the self is
redolent of the Old Testament in which anthropological concepts
tend to denote the whole person rather than specific component
parts (TNT I, p. 196). *Sōma* is used in such a way that it could equally
well be translated by 'self' as by body. When Paul urges the Romans
to present their bodies (*sōmata*) as a living sacrifice, holy and
acceptable to God, he is referring to the whole person (cf. 1 Cor
9:27; 13:3; Rom 6:12ff.; Phil 1:20). Even in 1 Corinthians 15, where
Paul, in arguing with his opponents, tends to use *sōma* to refer to the
physical body, we still encounter the underlying idea that human
existence is somatic. Consequently, the resurrection from the dead
continues to be thought of as bodily existence.

The theological significance of *sōma* resides in the way in which
people are related to themselves. As such, human beings are both the
subjects and objects of their own actions. I can determine what I
make of myself and in this relationship to myself my freedom and
responsibility as a creature reside. This existential fact creates the
double possibility of fulfilment or alienation; somatic existence can
be either for or against God (TNT I, p. 196). This, moreover, is a
temporal possibility; it is always directed toward the future and, as
possibility, it is never a permanent possession.

Bultmann's analysis of *sōma* is confirmed by his analysis of the
terms *psychē* (soul), *pneuma* (spirit), and *zōē* (life). Like *sōma*, these
do not refer to specific parts or aspects of human existence; they
refer to the way in which human beings are related to themselves
(TNT I, pp. 203–10). *Pneuma*, used as an anthropological term, is
to be carefully distinguished from its theological use in reference to
the Spirit of God. As an anthropological term it can often be translated by a personal pronoun. Thus, when Paul says 'they refreshed
my spirit (*pneuma*) as well as yours' (1 Cor 16:18), he could just as
well have said 'they refeshed me as well as you' (TNT I, p. 206).

If the foregoing categories contain Paul's ontology, it is also true
that he makes ontic statements about the estrangement of all human
existence. He asserts not only the possibility of fallenness but its
actuality for all people. The claim of God the Creator is upon all

persons but this is a claim that has been wilfully disregarded. This is the force of the expression 'according to the flesh' (*kata sarka*) when used as a modifier of verbs (TNT I, p. 237). 'Those who live according to the flesh set their minds on the things of the flesh' (Rom 8:5). The sphere of 'flesh' involves not only sins of sensuality (Gal 5:24), but also boasting in works of the law (Phil 3:3). It is clear that Bultmann reads Paul's understanding of 'flesh' in the light of the human condition alienated from God.

> The sinful self-delusion that one lives out of the created world can manifest itself both in unthinking recklessness (this especially among the Gentiles) and in considered busy-ness (this especially among Jews)—both in the ignoring or transgressing of ethical demands and in excessive zeal to fulfil them. For the sphere of 'flesh' is by no means just the life of instinct or sensual passions, but is just as much that of the moral and religious efforts of man. (TNT I, p. 239)

The domain of sin is also the domain of death. This is apparent in the much debated passage at Romans 7:7-25. According to Bultmann, Paul is not so much describing his own guilt-racked past as looking at the human condition under the law from the standpoint of Christian faith. The Law which was given for life has become the instrument of death (v. 10), and those who seek to live according to the flesh are already under the dispensation of death. Consequently, this world (*kosmos*) is characterized by its opposition to God's reign. It is the world of human activity marked by false wisdom and piety, and also a world of ungodly powers in which human beings are held captive (TNT I, p. 256).

Central to Paul's description of existence prior to faith is his understanding of the law (TNT I, pp. 259-69). In the law of the Old Testament, God's demand is encountered. The law is given by God's grace and it is intended that human beings live in obedience to it. According to Bultmann, the 'law' in Paul refers usually to the totality of ritual and ethical demands found in the Torah, although his emphasis rests upon the ethical. The situation of the Gentiles is analogous in that the ethical demands of the law are present through conscience (Rom 2:15).

Prior to faith in Christ, there is no genuine fulfilment of the law (Rom 3:9). Both Jews and Gentiles are under the power of sin. Yet it is not even intended that human beings should achieve salvation in this way. To attempt to be justified by works of the law is already to have gone astray (Gal 2:6). Justification is by God's grace given in Christ. 'Christ is the end of the law, that every one who has faith may be justified' (Rom 10:4).

> Justification by works of the Law and justification by divine grace appropriated in man's faith exclude each other. (TNT I, p. 263)

While the law brings to light human sinfulness, Paul, according to Bultmann, does not claim that the law leads to crisis and despair. The law does not become, for the Jew, an unbearable burden which leads to the threshold of faith in the gospel. This function of the law, which is prominent in Luther,[12] is not found in Bultmann's interpretation of Paul. Certainly, the law serves the gospel of Christ insofar as it exposes the objective situation of the sinner on hearing the gospel. Nonetheless, it does not do this by provoking a subjective crisis in the heart of the sinner struggling to conform to the Law. The law, indeed, remains in force for the believer as 'the law of Christ' (Gal 6:2) and through the Spirit it is possible that the law may be fulfilled in us (Rom 8:4) (TNT I, p. 268).

Bultmann's understanding of the Old Testament is dominated by his conception of the relationship between law and gospel. Insofar as the grace of God in Jesus Christ cannot be understood apart from our sinfulness under God's law, the Old Testament is a necessary presupposition for the New. In its presentation of the moral demands of God, the Hebrew Scriptures must always stand alongside the Christian witness. Where the law is not understood, the gospel will be distorted and cheapened.

> [M]an must stand under the Old Testament if he wants to understand the New. The material connection between Law and Gospel means that the Gospel can be preached only when man stands under the Law. Certainly, Christ is the end of the Law; but precisely so that he can be understood as the end of the Law (otherwise Christ is not understood at all), everyone who hears of him must also have heard of the Law. More than that: he must hear the Law again and again.[13]

Bultmann qualifies this evaluation of the Old Testament in a number of ways. He claims that the moral demands of the Old Testament, unlike the cultic, are enduring and remain valid. These, however, are not peculiar to Judaism and are embodied in other conceptions of the divine law. These others, in fact, might equally well function as the presupposition of the Gospel.[14] There are, however, further affinities between the Old and the New Testaments. The conception of human existence as particular and historical is common to Judaism and Christianity. The idea that all human life stands under the sovereign rule of the Creator is also common to both faiths and, in this respect, the Old Testament continues to speak to the Christian community.

We must also reckon with the fact that, for the Old Testament, the Torah is itself a gift of God's grace and a sign of God's call to human beings. It is grace that constitutes God's relationship with Israel and provides the basis for obedience under the law. This grace however is linked to the history of a specific people and, within that history, it gradually assumes an eschatological character. The fortunes of the people are no longer taken as the present reality of grace. Instead the manifestation of that grace is 'transferred to an eschatological future' (PCCS, p. 56). In the light of the Christian claim that this eschatological event has become a present reality for all nations in the death of Jesus, the religion of the Old Testament is superseded. Its abiding significance for Bultmann is located primarily in its setting of the demands of the law alongside the proclamation of the grace of Jesus Christ. To that extent, the Old Testament stands in a necessary dialectical relationship to the New.

This analysis of the Old Testament is buttressed by Bultmann's interpretation of first-century Judaism. Here he tends toward the view that rabbinic Judaism is generally legalist in its theological outlook, and thus sets up a religion of works. This provides the immediate background to Paul's doctrine of justification and enables a sharp contrast between faith and works to be drawn. Of rabbinic Judaism, Bultmann concludes,

> In the end the whole range of man's relation with God came to be thought of in terms of merit, including faith itself. (PCCS, p. 71)

The use of the word 'merit' is sufficient to intimate the Lutheran doctrine of justification that is about to be presented in Bultmann's interpretation of Paul.

Existence under faith

According to Paul, justification, *dikaiosynē*, is the presupposition of the Christian life. It is not so much the fact of justification as the manner in which it is realized that separates him from Judaism. Literally, justification is a term which describes the condition for obtaining salvation but it is so inextricably tied to it that it becomes almost synonymous with the essence of salvation (TNT I, p. 271). Bultmann is adamant that, for Paul, justification is a forensic (legal) term which denotes the acknowledgement of a person as righteous. It does not refer to an ethical quality so much as an authoritative declaration that a person is righteous. As a forensic term, it also becomes an eschatological term in Judaism; it refers to God's final verdict in the day of judgement. 'Blessed are those who hunger and thirst for righteousness' (Matt 5:6). Justification is thus to be understood relationally rather than substantively. It denotes a relation that is established by the action of God rather than a property possessed by human beings.

According to Bultmann, one major difference between Paul and Judaism is that, for Paul, this 'forensic eschatological righteousness' is already imputed to the believer in the present (TNT I, p. 274). God's eschatological judgement has already been announced and the believer can anticipate the future in confidence. 'Since, therefore, we are now justified by his blood, much more shall we be saved by him' (Rom 5:9). In Romans 5 - 8 we find Paul struggling to express this idea, that God's eschatological verdict has already been pronounced, alongside the notion that the fulfilment of the creation still lies in the future. The cosmic drama that is still awaited can only be the 'completion and confirmation' of what has already happened (TNT I, p. 306).

A further difference with Judaism is that, for Paul, justification is attained not through works of the law but through faith in Christ. This faith has its basis in the grace of God which justifies the guilty sinner. The doctrine of justification brings to light the two alternative possibilities of human existence: to live by works or to live by faith in Christ. The abuse of the law is simply a particular expression of the inauthentic existence that marks all human life prior to faith.

> A specifically human striving has merely taken on its culturally, and in point of time, individually distinct form in Judaism. For it is, in fact, a striving common to all men, to gain recognition of one's achievement; and this generates pride.[15]

The faith by which justification is appropriated has the character of passive submission to the love of God, as opposed to the active doing of good works (TNT I, p. 314). This faith also displays the character of knowledge since it is focused upon the death and resurrection of

Christ as the salvation occurrence. These two are bound together for Paul, and cannot be separated. For Bultmann, it is significant that Paul's theology is concentrated upon the crucifixion of Jesus, rather than upon the earthly ministry which preceded it.

> Jesus' death-and-resurrection, then, is for Paul the decisive thing about the person of Jesus and his life experience, indeed, in the last analysis it is the sole thing of importance for him—implicitly included are the incarnation and earthly life of Jesus as bare facts. That is, Paul is interested only in the *fact* that Jesus became man and lived on earth. *How* he was born or lived interests him only to the extent of knowing that Jesus was a definite, concrete man, a Jew, 'being born in the likeness of man and being born under the law.' (Gal 4:4) But beyond that, Jesus' manner of life, his ministry, his personality, his character play no role at all. (TNT I, p. 294)

In the light of this, we can understand why the quest of the historical Jesus is theologically irrelevant. The salvation occurrence is identified with the death and resurrection of Jesus, and not with the details of his preceding ministry. The question still remains, however, why Paul believed that this death was of salvific significance. Bultmann shows the way in which Paul elucidates the crucifixion by reference to a range of borrowed motifs: propitiatory sacrifice, vicarious sacrifice, redemption, the dying and rising of the mystery religions, and the Gnostic myth of descent and ascent (TNT I, pp. 295ff.). The proliferation of these motifs indicates that Paul was dissatisfied with all explanations of the death of Jesus which dealt in terms of mythical or metaphysical categories. The death of Jesus is not to be understood in terms of a theory but only existentially. Christ can only be known as 'the Son of God who loved me and gave himself for me' (Gal 2:20). It is only as I know myself personally determined by his death and resurrection that I understand that significance. It is not that I first understand the theory about the death of Jesus and then, secondly, surrender myself to God. Faith is a single act in which I am brought into a new relationship with God and the saving truth of the cross. There is no way of understanding the death of Jesus other than by being apprehended by God's word.

> [T]he salvation occurrence is nowhere present except in the proclaiming, accosting, demanding, and promising word of preaching. (TNT I, p. 302)

It is only as a new possibility of existence is realized through the word of the cross that I can understand its theological meaning. Here we see the harmony between Bultmann's own existential approach and his Pauline interpretation. The justification of the sinner through faith in Christ is realized in the discovery of a new possibility of existence. This new mode of being is marked by a trust in God's love and a commitment to life in the Spirit. It is a life of freedom from anxiety in which I am enabled to love my neighbour in response to God's love (TNT I, pp. 330ff.). It is distinguished by freedom: freedom from the power of death and the sufferings of this life. In accepting suffering, the Christian, at the same time, displays victory over it, for by sharing in the fellowship of Christ's sufferings the Christian witnesses to his resurrection. 'While we live we are always being given up to death for Jesus' sake, so that the life of Jesus may be manifested in our mortal flesh' (2 Cor 4:11).

The influence of Heidegger and Luther

Ernst Käsemann, the Tübingen New Testament scholar, is one of Bultmann's most distinguished pupils, yet we find in his work an important critique of Bultmann's treatment of Pauline anthropology. According to Käsemann, Bultmann's analysis of the concept of *sōma* betrays the influence of Heidegger and is symptomatic of a more general distortion of Paul's theology. He argues that the concept *sōma* appears frequently in Paul with strong physicalist overtones and to translate it into the modern concept of the self is to misconstrue Paul's meaning. The parallelism of 'body' and 'flesh', the emphasis upon the resurrection of the body, the offering of our bodies as our spiritual worship, and the obviously physical dimension to the claim that 'the body is not meant for immorality, but for the Lord' (1 Cor 6:13)—all these suggest that Bultmann is forcing an unwarranted meaning upon the text.[16]

This criticism is mirrored by the claim that, in his doctrine of justification, Bultmann is preoccupied by the existential state of the justified sinner and, consequently, fails to make sense of Paul's theological claims about the God who justifies. For Käsemann, the Pauline concept of justification cannot be divorced from the being of God. Justification must be understood not only as denoting a relational state, but also as referring to the being and action of God. According to Paul, the power of God is active within us, the Spirit is given to us, and Christ lives in us.[17] By thinking of justification in relation to these strands of Pauline thought we set it within its proper theological, Christological and eschatological context. These dimensions of justification are overlooked by Bultmann in his exclusively relational treatment of the problem. The result is a shift towards an excessively individualistic anthropology which obscures the lordship of God over the created order, and the eschatological tension in which the Christian must live.[18]

Käsemann's criticisms are part of a wider theological attack upon Bultmann. Pauline thought is not to be cashed out in terms of two fundamental possibilities of existence that confront the isolated individual. The human situation must be understood not existentially but historically and theologically. The human being is embedded in the physical world and is subject to political and social forces. Human possibilities cannot be understood apart from the situation of the whole created order in relation to its Creator who has been revealed in the history of a people. Bultmann's exclusive focus upon the detached human subject confronting two possibilities of existence reflects an uncritical allegiance to Heidegger's anthropology.

> It is significant for both hermeneutics and systematic theology that Bultmann (under Heidegger's influence) conceives human reality primarily as possibility, whereas Paul at most sees possibility as a manifestation of reality and always assigns to the body the reality of creatureliness, the reality of the fall, of redemption, of the resurrection of the dead, with all of which the appropriate functions are associated.[19]

A further, and even more extensive, critique of Bultmann's Pauline interpretation can be found in a succession of recent attempts to 'de-Lutheranize' Paul. The notion that Paul understood human existence in terms of a dialectic between works-righteousness and faith-righteousness has been called into question by a variety of arguments. The most significant single contribution has been that of E.P. Sanders in *Paul and Palestinian Judaism*. Sanders has attempted to show that it is an egregious error to treat first-century Judaism as a religion of works, and he has argued that Bultmann was led astray by an uncritical acceptance of the conclusions of Schürer and Bousset.[20] Bultmann's presentation of first-century Judaism, especially in *Primitive Christianity in its Contemporary Setting*, shows little direct knowledge of the primary literature, especially rabbinic sources, and his adoption of Schürer and Bousset makes no attempt even to acknowledge the work of their critics.

Bultmann's interpretation of Judaism thus leans heavily towards legalism, and paves the way for his Lutheran dialectic of faith and works.[21]

In rabbinic religion, Sanders argues, it is clear that God has graciously chosen Israel and has given her the law. The law is commanded by God for the proper maintenance of the covenant relationship, yet it is nowhere said that obedience to the law merits God's election. While individuals may transgress and be excluded from the covenant community, it is not suggested that the covenant itself can be revoked. Moreover, for those who transgress, God has provided means of atonement.

In the light of this understanding of first-century Judaism (which Paul shares) Sanders concludes that Bultmann has misunderstood the apostle. The notion that 'boasting in one's own achievements' constitutes Paul's attack upon Judaism is a fundamental error. The Lutheran approach which schematizes Paul's theology in terms of the human predicament and the divine solution distorts what is said there about Judaism. For Paul, salvation is to be found through faith in Christ. The covenant with Israel has now been superseded, and, consequently, the law is no longer the primary vehicle of God's grace. This is the centre of Paul's theology. His polemic against the law is directed not against a religion of works but against an alternative conception of God's grace. Commenting on Bultmann's analysis, Sanders writes:

> Penetrating as this is, and persuasively as it is put, I should say that it is wrong by being backwards. It is not Paul's analysis of the nature of sin which determines his view, but his analysis of the way to salvation; not his anthropology, but his Christology and soteriology. . . . The contrast, in other words, is not between self-reliance and reliance on God—two kinds of self-understanding—but between belonging to Christ and not belonging to Christ.[22]

According to Sanders, Bultmann has understood the solution in terms of the plight. Whereas the centre of Paul's thought lies in his Christology, Bultmann has located it in his anthropology. It is the work of Christ and the relationship of the believer to him that is fundamental for Paul, not two possible modes of existence. In the light of this exegetical disagreement, Sanders cannot avoid drawing the conclusion that Bultmann's predilection for 'existentialist demythologizing' has led him astray in his interpretation of Paul.[23]

The current debate about Paul and the law is highly complex not least because there are a variety of positions being adopted, rather than simply two polar interpretations.[24] Bultmann, as we have already seen, is not totally tied to a traditional Lutheran position. He claims, against Luther, that Paul did not suffer from an anxiety-ridden conscience in his efforts to live according to the law. The law is not given in order to provoke human despair and to lead the sinner toward the gospel. But is Sanders correct in claiming that Bultmann 'proceeded from plight to solution and supposed that Paul proceeded in the same way'?[25]

Bultmann, in various places, argues that Paul's description of human alienation from God is governed by his new understanding of existence under faith. In this respect, Bultmann's approach is faithful to Paul in perceiving the manner in which the doctrine of justification is Christologically controlled. But can Bultmann's claim, that Paul understands human existence prior to faith primarily in terms of justification by works as opposed to grace, survive Sanders's attack? We might attempt to respond along the following lines.[26]

Sanders has undoubtedly demonstrated the manner in which election, covenant and grace are dominant themes in first-century Judaism. Yet this does not preclude the possibility that in Paul there is a radicalizing of the concepts of sin and grace which leads to a break with Judaism. As a Christian, Paul inherited the belief that Christ died for our sins (1 Cor 15:3; Rom 5:8). This belief implies a judgement on the human condition as estranged from God and guilty of sin. Hence we find in the opening chapters of the letter to the Romans the thesis that all human existence, Jewish and Gentile, is cursed by sin. Since all have transgressed the demands of the law, the law cannot be the pathway to life as it was for the Old Testament (Rom 3:23; 9:31; Gal 3:10). Justification is now exclusively focused upon the death of Christ once for all to the explicit exclusion of any reference to obedience to the law. This is not to attribute to Judaism a belief in works-righteousness but it is to present a more radical view of grace and of the justification of the ungodly. While Paul himself is not unconcerned with Christian obedience to God's law, this obedience is made possible through the work of the Spirit which further reflects his more intense emphasis upon divine grace.

Although Paul's theological position is determined by his Christology rather than by a conviction of Jewish legalism, this does not imply that the doctrine of justification, which subsequently arises out of that Christology, is invalid. Sanders's criticism that 'the solution preceded the plight' does not seem to warrant dismissal of Paul's description of the plight. Furthermore, if Paul's position is largely determined by the particular circumstances of his controversy with Jewish Christianity, this does not prevent the theology which issues from these circumstances having universal applicability.

On the other hand, it is not clear that Bultmann's position can survive unscathed. For Bultmann, Pauline theology is to be cashed out in terms of two fundamental possibilities of existence. Yet Sanders and others seem to have shown that the centre of Paul's thought lies not in an understanding of human existence but in a belief about what Christ has achieved through his death and resurrection. At the centre of Pauline theology we have a Christology rather than an anthropology. The reduction of Paul's thought to a statement of the basic modes of existence betrays the influence of Heidegger. The focus has shifted from Christology to anthropology in a way that distorts Paul's intention.

In addition to this, we have to take into account that, for Paul, human existence is alienated from God because of the failure of all men and women to adhere to the demands of the law. Bultmann, however, has claimed that what Paul is really saying is that even to attempt to find salvation through works of the law represents a false understanding of existence. Yet we have suggested that neither Judaism nor Paul adopted this attitude towards the law. The problem is not the attempt to be obedient to the law but the failure to be so. Here again Bultmann's interpretation of Paul requires to be modified. It would seem that, for Paul, human failure to keep the law and the death of Christ as atonement for sin are more central than Bultmann allows. Instead of exposing the real subject matter (*Sache*) of Paul's thought, Bultmann's hermeneutical commitments are in danger of obscuring it.[27]

III. JOHN

Bultmann's interpretation of the fourth gospel is probably the outstanding achievement of his life's work. Anyone who has seriously studied his long commentary, *The Gospel of John*, cannot fail to be impressed by its wealth of insight and its profound concentration upon the subject matter of the text. In many ways, the fourth gospel is more responsive to Bultmann's hermeneutical strategy than any other book in the New Testament. The parables and sayings of the kingdom are almost entirely absent. The miracle stories and disputes are thoroughly integrated into the thematic constructions and symbolism of the long theological discourses. The monologues are not attempts to explain in either historical or metaphysical terms how we are justified in believing that Jesus is the revelation of God; instead, their intention is to witness to the fact that Jesus is the revealer, and to describe what it means to believe in him and his words.

Many of Bultmann's general conclusions regarding the fourth gospel represent opinions which have been widely held since the time of David Friedrich Strauss. The Evangelist was familiar with the synoptic tradition and the gospel form, yet his presentation of the life of Jesus is different in several important respects. The long theological discourses, which are deeply coloured by the Evangelist's symbolism, differ markedly from the disconnected incidents, the short sayings, and the parables of the kingdom that dominate the synoptics. Jesus is no longer presented as a rabbi or as a prophet, but as the revealer whom God has sent into the world. While the passion story in John may have common roots in the authentic tradition about the historical Jesus we cannot say this of the discourses which centre on the 'I am' sayings. All these assumptions are embedded in Bultmann's approach to the fourth gospel.

The Evangelist and his sources

Bultmann believed that the fourth gospel had drawn heavily upon Gnostic ideas and imagery. Gnosticism for Bultmann, following in the path of Reitzenstein and Bousset, refers to a loosely defined religious movement which predated Christianity. The Gnostics stressed that salvation was attained through knowledge (*gnōsis*) often derived from a heavenly redeemer figure. Its outlook was dominated by a cosmological dualism which contrasted the evil of the material world with the goodness of the spiritual world. By presenting Gnostic ideas as the common currency of the first-century thought world, Bultmann was able to perceive the influence of Gnosticism upon the fourth gospel. The Evangelist, however, in borrowing the language of the Gnostics uses it for his own theological purposes. Consequently, we can observe in the fourth gospel a demythologizing of Gnostic ideas, and in particular, a reworking of the myth of the Gnostic redeemer figure who has descended from heaven to earth. Bultmann in presenting this interpretation appeals to material from the Mandaean sect as evidence of a pre-Christian Gnosticism.[28]

The symbolic dualism of the Gnostics pervades the fourth gospel.

The contrasts between light and darkness, truth and falsehood, above and below, freedom and bondage, are all deployed in order to depict the significance of the historical individual, Jesus of Nazareth. The coming of Jesus presents the world with a radical choice between light and darkness. To choose Jesus is to walk in the light of life. To reject him is to condemn oneself to darkness, falsehood and death. Yet, for the Evangelist, it is not so much that the cosmos is divided into two realms as that the decision for or against Jesus will determine the nature of one's existence. The dualist symbolism of Gnosticism is used to denote the two fundamental possibilities of human existence before God. 'The cosmological dualism of Gnosticism has become in John a dualism of decision' (TNT II, p. 21; cf. GJ, p. 55).

The two possibilities of existence that are presented by the Evangelist correspond in essence, if not in form, to the Pauline contrast between righteousness according to works and righteousness according to faith. Bultmann believes that the Evangelist perceived this, even more clearly than Paul, as the essence of the kerygma. In the fourth gospel, the Jewish opponents of Jesus represent the false quest for self-security (TNT II, pp. 27ff.). Their use of the law and Jewish religious traditions alienates them from God's revelation. Instead of preparing them for the appearance of the Christ, the law has now become a source of boasting and security. In this respect, the Jews stand as the representatives of the worldly attitude which shrinks from the coming of Jesus, and which prefers the false comfort of familiar securities lying at one's disposal. Here again, Bultmann's interpretation is heavily indebted to Heideggerian categories. Nicodemus, a Pharisee, is confronted through Jesus by two possibilities of existence corresponding to flesh and spirit (John 3:1–15). The miracle of rebirth is the miracle of faith in which Nicodemus can surrender to the judgement and grace of God. This is a decision which lies with him and which determines his status before God. Those passages in John which suggest a doctrine of theological determinism or predestination must be understood in the light of one's awesome freedom to choose or to reject the claim of Jesus (GJ, pp. 133–43).

As in Paul, we see in the fourth gospel a critique of traditional patterns of eschatological thought. The eschaton is no longer conceived of as an event that lies in the future. It is an event that has already occurred in Christ and in human responses to him. Salvation and damnation are no longer interpreted as twin fates that await one on the day of judgement. To confess Jesus is already to possess eternal life. To reject him is already to live under the curse of darkness and death. This thorough demythologizing of a futurist eschatology is, for Bultmann, one of the theological gains of the fourth gospel. His commentary is punctuated with references to the appearance of Jesus as the eschatological event. As such, the revelation of God in Jesus is invested with an ultimate significance and the summons to Christian faith is decisive for all human beings.

> [T]he earlier naive eschatology of Jewish Christianity and Gnosticism has been abandoned, certainly not in favour of a spiritualising of the eschatological process to become a process within man's soul, but in favour of a radical understanding of Jesus' appearance as the eschatological event. This event puts an end to the old course of the world. As from now on there are only believers and unbelievers, so there are also now only saved and lost, those who have life and those who are in death. (GJ, p. 155)

There are, however, various passages in the fourth gospel which strongly suggest remnants of the older futurist eschatology (John 6:39, 40, 44, 54; 12:48). Bultmann argues, controversially, that these are not part of the original gospel but are the insertions of a later ecclesiastical editor who wished to retain elements of the older tradition. This editorial redaction extends to the reference to the sacrament in the section 6:51b–58b, a reference which modifies the Evangelist's intentional lack of emphasis upon the significance of the sacraments (GJ, pp. 218ff.).[29]

The first half of the gospel is dominated by the recounting of several miracles performed by Jesus. These are sometimes referred to as 'signs' (*sēmeia*). Bultmann argues that the Evangelist drew upon a source comprising an account of seven miracle stories. The references in 2:11 and 4:54 to the first and second signs that Jesus performed are adduced as evidence of this (GJ, pp. 113ff.). The Evangelist, however, uses this source critically. While his gospel testifies to the occurrence of these signs, they are presented as ambiguous. The identity of Jesus is not demonstrated by these miracles; they do not preclude the need for the radical decision of faith. In some cases they may precipitate faith (4.53), but in others they are the cause of misunderstanding (6:15), and grave offence (11:47) (TNT II, p. 45). There is thus an implicit critique of the source, in the manner in which it is deployed by the writer.

The theme of the gospel is the revelation of God in human flesh

(1:14). This, though, is a revelation which is hidden and offensive. To recognize and to accept it requires the abandonment of self. 'This Birth was hard and bitter agony for us, like Death, our death' (T.S. Eliot). The emphasis upon the person of Christ is stronger in the fourth gospel than anywhere else in the New Testament. In particular, the theological discourses, which have at their centre the 'I am' sayings, point to the person of the revealer. The identity of this revealer is paradoxical. On the one hand, the highest possible claims are made for him, yet, at the same time, he is nothing in himself, for he is entirely dependent upon his Father. 'I have come down from heaven, not to do my own will, but the will of him who sent me' (6:38) (TNT II, pp. 50ff.; cf. GJ, p. 227).

In the case of the discourses, Bultmann claims again that the writer is working with a borrowed source which is critically adapted (e.g. GJ, p. 132). His source theory thus works to the advantage of his theological interpretation. The writer is perceived to be demythologizing traditional material that he inherited, and to be faithful to his intentions we must understand the Johannine language existentially.

The work of Christ is described in terms of his incarnation, rather than merely his crucifixion, as in Paul. Nonetheless, for the fourth gospel, the crucifixion is the final and climactic event of the incarnate life. Death is the last demonstration of Jesus' obedience to the Father; the final act of his commission which signals his return to heavenly glory. By the ambivalent use of the verb 'to be lifted up' (*hypsōthēnai*) the Evangelist points to the significance of the crucifixion. 'I, when I am lifted up from the earth, will draw all men to myself' (12:32). Jesus describes his death as the supreme moment of his glorification (17:1), and in resonance with this the Evangelist compresses the events of resurrection, ascension and the giving of the Spirit into a period of about twenty-four hours.

The discourses demythologized

When we examine Bultmann's interpretation of the theological discourses, we find that their meaning is simply directed to the bare fact that Jesus is the revealer. The 'I am' sayings do not attempt to provide evidence for the person of Jesus. There is no attempt at historical demonstration or metaphysical proof. These sayings merely witness through the use of symbol to the single truth that Jesus is the one in whom God is revealed. This feature of the fourth gospel is peculiarly congenial to Bultmann's own rejection of objectivizing patterns of thought in theology.

> Thus it turns out in the end that Jesus as the Revealer of God *reveals nothing but that he is the Revealer*. . . . John, that is, in his Gospel presents only the fact (*das Dass*) of the Revelation without describing its content (*ihr Was*). (TNT II, p. 66)

As we have already seen, Bultmann believes that, in order to express the significance of Jesus, the Evangelist has drawn upon the terms of a Gnostic redeemer myth (GJ, p. 61). The Gnostic redeemer is sent into the world by God to impart knowledge which will enable the elect to obtain their eternal salvation in heaven. It is this myth which is employed by the Evangelist in his frequent language about the coming down of the Son from heaven. Yet unlike the Gnostics, John asserts that the word of God actually became flesh (1:14). The redeemer is a mortal human being and does not appear merely in the disguise of flesh. Moreover he does not offer cosmological secrets to the elect; he confronts all human beings with a radical decision between faith and unbelief.

Bultmann considers that the language of incarnation and of the mutual indwelling between the Father and the Son is to be interpreted existentially rather than metaphysically. The fourth gospel is not asserting a literal identity of being between Jesus and God; the force of its utterances points to Jesus as the one through whom God is to be heard and obeyed. The Evangelist is not in the business of constructing theological dogmas; his intention is to point to the existential significance of Jesus.

> All this is said not in order to provide the basis for a speculative Christology, but because his origin is grounded in *what he means for us*; whoever hears him, hears God, whose words he speaks (3:34; 17:8); whoever sees him, sees God (14:9). Thus the statement about his equality with God refers to the situation of those who hear and see him, and not to his own metaphysical nature. (GJ, p. 249)

How, then, does one recognize Jesus as the revealer? The answer presented by the Evangelist, as Bultmann reads him, is only in faith. By responding to the claim of Jesus in faith, the fact of his revelation can be understood. Accordingly, the event of revelation is best elucidated by describing the character of faith. Faith is marked by freedom in that the believer is set free from self, and free to love others. The eschatological freedom of faith must be continually appropriated and, thereby, believers are aware of themselves as new creatures opened toward the future by the love of God (GJ, p. 440). There is an inner unity between faith and love in the fourth gospel in which the hearing and the doing of Jesus' words coincide. 'By this my Father is glorified, that you bear much fruit, and so prove to be my disciples' (John 15:8) (GJ, pp. 529ff.). Eschatological existence is also characterized by peace and joy. In resting upon the work of Christ the believer is finally set at peace, although this is a peace that sets one at odds with the world (ibid., p. 593). No longer in bondage to the cares and anxieties of this world, the believer can now live joyfully in the assurance that prayer will be heard (ibid., p. 585).

Historical and theological objections

Bultmann's interpretation of the fourth gospel is a masterly combination of exegetical criticism and theological construction. In many respects, his evaluation of the theology of the Evangelist recalls Søren Kierkegaard's *Philosophical Fragments* with its emphasis upon the paradox of the incarnation, the offence it causes, and its bare facticity which can only be established in faith.[30] At the same time, the thorough integration of theological, historical and textual argument makes Bultmann's commentary difficult to assess. Unlike many other commentaries, there is no general introduction which presents the overall hypothesis governing the writer's exegesis. The critic is required to construct Bultmann's general approach from his treatment of particular passages, and then to attempt a general evaluation.[31]

It is clear, however, that Bultmann's interpretation of the theological intentions of the Evangelist is, in large measure, dependent upon his belief that he inherited several sources which were subsequently amended, and later edited, in the composition of the gospel. Thus the claim that the Evangelist is demythologizing the Gnostic redeemer myth depends, in part, upon there being in circulation at that time Gnostic literature depicting the descent and ascent of the heavenly redeemer. Similarly, the belief that the Evangelist is dehistoricizing the traditional eschatology is contingent upon the theory that various futurist eschatological verses are the product of editorial insertion. The relative lack of emphasis ascribed to the Evangelist's treatment of miracles is conditioned by the hypothesis of the *sēmeia* source, and the claim that the revelatory discourses are to be interpreted existentially, rather than metaphysically, likewise depends on the belief that the Evangelist inherited, rather than composed, these discourses.

While it is not possible to discuss in any detail this array of hypotheses it must be said that each of them has proved controversial. Evidence for an elaborate and systematic form of pre-Christian Gnosticism is uncertain. While there are signs of Gnostic imagery in the Qumran documents there is little evidence of the Gnostic redeemer figure. Bultmann's appeal to the Mandaean literature cannot now be taken to demonstrate conclusively the hypothesis. The Mandaeans were an Iranian baptizing sect who claimed to originate from John the Baptist. Yet it now appears that the Mandaean documents were re-edited after the rise of Christianity and reflect anti-Christian polemic. They cannot, therefore, be taken as a reliable guide to the Gnostic roots of the fourth gospel. On the other hand, the Gnostic influence upon John cannot be discounted.[32]

Bultmann's thesis regarding the insertions of the redactor, enslaved to traditional patterns of thought, has failed to command much support. The idea that believers remain dependent upon the power of God to raise them up 'on the last day' is thought by many commentators to be integral to Johannine theology.[33] Moreover, the references to future eschatology seem to be more extensive than Bultmann recognizes and, given the eschatological nature of early Christianity, it seems unlikely that the Evangelist could have departed from it altogether. In the light of John 14:2-3; 17:24; 12:25-26, Eduard Schweizer concludes

It is surely not true to say that John expected from the future nothing more than what is already present for the believer.[34]

There are also doubts about the source hypotheses that Bultmann brings to bear upon his interpretation of Johannine theology. While the enumeration of the first and second signs may suggest a borrowed source, there is an absence of any further enumeration. The particular term 'sign' may suggest a source of 'signs', but not all the miracles narrated in the gospel are specifically designated as signs.[35] Thus, while there may be some evidence in favour of a signs source, its probability has not been convincingly demonstrated. The hypothesis of a revelatory discourse source looks much less probable. The Johannine style pervades the theological discourses, and the manner in which these discourses are so thoroughly intertwined with the narrative material suggests more the original work of the

Evangelist (or someone with whom he was in contact) than the deployment of traditional discourse material.[36]

In the light of these critical observations, we must raise questions of Bultmann's assessment of the theological intentions of the Evangelist. The proposals concerning the Gnostic redeemer myth and the source of revelatory discourses support his thesis that the fourth gospel is to be read existentially rather than metaphysically. Yet this would appear to be a modern distinction which the Evangelist himself would not have recognized, and it is doubtful whether the text can easily be made to support it. If the theological discourses and the redemption myth are central to the Evangelist's presentation of the identity of Jesus, we must ask whether Christology, rather than anthropology, is at the heart of the fourth gospel. The question mark against Bultmann's Pauline interpretation reappears against his Johannine interpretation.

The Evangelist is making statements about the being of Jesus Christ and not merely about his existential significance for believers. These are not mutually exclusive as Bultmann would have it but are mutually implied.[37] The incarnational statement of the Prologue (1:14) implies the importance of the historical life of Jesus as the locus of revelation and not merely as a signal of its paradoxical nature. Rather than as the adaptation of uncongenial source material, we might try to see the fourth gospel as an attempt to think through the question of the person of Christ in a cosmological and metaphysical direction (already begun by Paul and the writer of Hebrews), while at the same time remaining faithful to the synoptic tradition.[38]

The fact that the writer of the fourth gospel has selected the gospel genre as his medium is itself significant. In particular, the recounting of the passion, crucifixion and resurrection narratives indicates that these are indispensable for understanding the claims made in the gospel about the person of Jesus as the incarnate Logos, the only-begotten Son of the Father. The narrative material is not therefore to be translated out into an existential message, since it is theologically necessary for understanding the claims that are made by the Evangelist.

These criticisms notwithstanding, Bultmann's commentary remains a masterpiece of New Testament scholarship. The very fact that it is cited extensively by most subsequent commentaries indicates that it is one of the landmarks in the field. It is perhaps above all its fusion of theological insight and critical exegesis which mark it out as one of the great commentaries on the fourth gospel; its combination of historical scholarship and devotional fervour makes it almost unique. The treatment of the Farewell Discourses and the trial of Jesus before Pilate are profoundly moving, and anyone who reads Bultmann's comments on these passages will return to John's gospel with fresh perception and a conviction of the commentary's lasting worth.

In our exploration of Bultmann's interpretation of the New Testament we have seen the extent to which his historical and theological proposals are intertwined. The assertion that Paul and John are already engaged in demythologizing eschatological and Gnostic concepts indicates the extent to which demythologizing is an integral feature of Bultmann's theology of the New Testament. In the light of this, we can now set the famous demythologizing controversy of the 1940s and 1950s in the context of Bultmann's theology as a whole.

Notes

1 *Die Geschiche der synoptischen Tradition* (Göttingen, 1921) was largely written during Bultmann's time in Breslau, and predates dialectical theology. *History of the Synoptic Tradition* (London, 1972) is a translation of the 3rd German edition (1931).

2 For a useful introduction and critique of the methods of form criticism see John Muddiman, 'Form criticism' in R.J. Coggins and J.L. Houlden (eds), *Dictionary of Biblical Interpretation* (London, 1990), pp. 240-3; E.V. McKnight, *What is Form Criticism?* (Philadelphia, 1969).

3 For Bultmann's discussion of the methods of form criticism and the relation of his work to the earlier form-critical work of Martin Dibelius see 'The materials and the task', HST, pp. 1-7; 'The new approach to the synoptic problem' (1926), EF, pp. 39-62.

4 For a helpful summary of Bultmann's findings see E.V. McKnight, pp. 25-37.

5 J. Stevenson (ed.), *A New Eusebius* (London, 1983), p. 50.

6 Cf. Stephen Travis on 'the axioms of form criticism' in 'Form criticism' in I.H. Marshall (ed.), *New Testament Interpretation* (Exeter, 1977), pp. 153-5.

7 This circular method is noted by Bultmann himself. 'The forms of the literary tradition must be used to establish the influences operating in the life of the community, and the life of the community must be used to render the forms themselves intelligible': HST, p. 5.

8 Cf. Travis, p. 158.

9 Cf. Graham Stanton, 'Form criticism' in M.D. Hooker and C. Hickling (ed.), *What About the New Testament?* (London, 1975), pp. 20ff.

10 For a critique of the criterion of dissimilarity see R.S. Barbour, *Traditio-Historical Criticism of the Gospels* (London, 1972), Part 1, pp. 1-27.

11 G. Stanton, *The Gospels and Jesus* (Oxford, 1989), ch. 9, pp. 150-64.

12 Cf. Gerhard Ebeling, 'The twofold use of the law' in *Luther* (London, 1972), pp. 125-40.

13 'Die Bedeutung des Alten Testaments für den christlichen Glauben' (1933); 'The significance of the Old Testament for Christian faith' in B.W. Anderson (ed.), *The Old Testament and Christian Faith* (London, 1964), p. 15.

14 Ibid., p. 17.

15 'Christus des Gesetzes Ende' (1940); 'Christ the end of the law', EPT, p. 43.

16 Ernst Käsemann, 'On Paul's anthropology' in *Perspectives on Paul* (London, 1971), pp. 18ff.

17 Ernst Käsemann, ' ''The righteousness of God'' in Paul' in *New Testament Questions of Today* (London, 1969), p. 174.

18 Ibid., pp. 180-2. For Bultmann's response to Käsemann see '*dikaiosynē Theou*', Ex, pp. 470-5; for further responses in defence of Bultmann's 'individualism' see G. Bornkamm, *Paul* (New York, 1971), pp. 146ff., and Hans Conzelmann, *Outline of the Theology of the New Testament* (London, 1969), p. 172.

19 'On Paul's anthropology', p. 19.

20 Emil Schürer, *History of the Jewish People* (5 vols; Edinburgh, 1885-91); W. Bousset, *Die Religion des Judentums in späthellenistischen Zeitalter* (3rd ed, 1926).

21 E.P. Sanders, *Paul and Palestinian Judaism* (London, 1977), pp. 43f.

22 Ibid., pp. 481-2. Sanders's work has been echoed and developed by others. Francis Watson, in his impressive sociological study *Paul, Judaism and Gentiles* (Cambridge, 1986), argues that Paul's treatment of the law is to be understood in terms of the peculiar historical situation in which he found himself, in relation to Jewish Christianity. Paul's arguments, in Watson's study, appear more as the *ad hominem* claims of a sectarian doing violence to his opponents' position.

    The fundamental antithesis between faith and works is not to be understood as a primarily theological contrast between receiving salvation as a free gift and earning it by one's own efforts, but as a sociological contrast between two different ways of life: 'faith', the way of life practised in the Pauline congregations, marked by the abandonment of certain of the norms and beliefs of the surrounding society, and the adoption of new norms and beliefs; and 'works', the way of the life of the Jewish community, which sought to live in conformity with the law of Moses. The two are incompatible not because one stresses grace and the other achievement, but because the law is not observed in the Pauline congregations. (pp. 178–9)

23 Sanders, p. 454.

24 For an excellent guide to the current state of the debate see Stephen Westerholm, *Israel's Law and the Church's Faith* (Grand Rapids, 1988), Part 1, pp. 15–101.

25 Sanders, p. 442.

26 I am following here the argument of Westerholm, Part 2, pp. 105–222.

27 These last two criticisms of Bultmann can be found in Ulrich Wilckens, 'Christologie und Anthropologie im Zusammenhang der paulinischen Rechtfertigungslehre', *Zeitschrift für die neutestamentliche Wissenschaft* 67 (1976), pp. 64–82. On the basis of passages such as 1 Cor 1:30; 6:1; 2 Cor 5:21, Wilckens argues that Paul's doctrine of justification is grounded in Christology. The death of Christ as an atonement for sin is the context in which the sinner is justified and sins forgiven. Even in Romans faith does not lose its focus upon the death and resurrection of Christ. It is this which is the true object of faith and which provides the ground for Christian existence. A similar critique of Bultmann can be found in Eduard Schweizer, 'Zur Interpretation des Kreuzes bei R. Bultmann' in *Aux Sources de la Tradition Chrétienne* (Neuchâtel, 1950), pp. 228–38.

28 This approach was outlined in the earlier essay, 'Die Bedeutung der neuerschlossenen mandäischen und manichäischen Quellen für das Verständis des Johannesevangeliums' (1925), Ex, pp. 55–104. For an overview of Bultmann's understanding of Gnosticism see his *Gnosis* (London, 1952), the translation of his article in Kittel's *Theologisches Wörterbuch zum Neuen Testament*.

29 See also the earlier essay 'Die Eschatologie des Johannesevangelium' (1928); 'The eschatology of the gospel of John', FU, pp. 165–83.

30 Søren Kierkegaard, *Philosophical Fragments* (Princeton, 1974).

31 For an overall construction and analysis of Bultmann's understanding of the fourth gospel see D.M. Smith, *The Composition and Order of the Fourth Gospel: Bultmann's Literary Theory* (London, 1965).

32 For a critique of Bultmann's views on the Gnostic influence cf. Rudolf Schnackenburg, *The Gospel According to St. John* I (London, 1968), pp. 138–49, 543–57; C.H. Dodd, *The Interpretation of the Fourth Gospel* (Cambridge, 1953), pp. 97–130; R.McL. Wilson, 'The Gnostic heresy in the light of recent research and discovery' in *Gnosis and the New Testament* (Oxford, 1968), pp. 1–30. Bultmann's hypothesis still commands qualified support in e.g. Helmut Koester, 'Early Christianity from the perspective of the history of religions: Rudolf

Bultmann's contribution' in E.C. Hobbs (ed.), *Bultmann: Retrospect and Prospect* (Philadelphia, 1985), pp. 59-74; Walter Schmithals, *Neues Testament und Gnosis* (Darmstadt, 1988).

33 Cf. C.K. Barrett, *The Gospel According to St John* (2nd ed., London, 1978), pp. 69f., 283f.

34 E. Schweizer, *Jesus* (London, 1971), p. 165.

35 Cf. Barrett, pp. 18ff. For a defence of 'the signs source' see R.T. Fortna, *The Gospel of Signs* (Cambridge, 1970).

36 For a further critique of Bultmann's source theory see D.M. Smith, *Johannine Christianity* (Columbia, 1984), pp. 39-61.

37 Cf. Ernst Käsemann, *The Testament of Jesus* (London, 1968), p. 25.

38 This alternative hypothesis is raised by C.F. Evans in his article review of GJ in *Scottish Journal of Theology* 26 (1973), pp. 341-9; cf. R. Schnackenburg, pp. 553-7.

6

The demythologizing programme

From 1941 onwards Bultmann's name was associated with the notorious catchword 'demythologizing' (*Entmythologisierung*). The original demythologizing essay has been described as 'perhaps the single most discussed and controversial theological writing of the century'.[1] Yet rather than constituting a new departure in his theology the demythologizing essays merely reiterated formal and material claims that were familiar to those already acquainted with Bultmann's work. Before examining its contents it is worth pausing to consider the ecclesial and political context of the original 1941 essay, 'New Testament and Mythology'.[2]

The essay was originally presented as a paper at two conferences of ministers belonging to the Confessing Church. The paper was intended to stimulate discussion within the Confessing Church, which Bultmann believed was in danger of slipping into a narrow and outmoded orthodoxy. As he later said in a letter to Jochen Niemöller, the witness of the Church requires not only courage but intellectual clarity.[3] Its intention was not merely the negative one of exposing the archaic world-view of the New Testament. Bultmann wished to reiterate his positive conviction that the word of God could not be identified with the phenomena of this world. The political implications of this were made clear in a companion essay which initially appeared alongside 'New Testament and Mythology'.[4] In this essay, 'The Question of Natural Revelation', Bultmann claimed that historical phenomena were ambiguous and could not be employed as criteria for theological truth.

Every phenomenon of history is ambiguous, and none reveals God's will in itself; and now more than ever every historical phenomenon of the present is ambiguous . . . The essential nature of the German people is not present as a clear criterion by virtue of which we may clearly judge the rightness of action. The judgment must run to the effect that man in the face of God is a sinner, and that his history is a history of sinful men, and therefore in actual fact enshrouds God in a veil.[5]

It was unfortunate that the original ecclesial and political context of Bultmann's demythologizing essay was neglected in the ensuing controversy. The negative and iconoclastic impressions created might well have been avoided had Bultmann's intentions been borne in mind. The demythologizing programme reflects the combination of modern criticism and faithfulness to the Christian tradition that we have found everywhere else in Bultmann's theology.[6]

The New Testament world-view and existential interpretation

According to Bultmann, the writings that comprise the New Testament are deeply infected by a first-century world-view which is no longer tenable. The universe is a three-storey structure in which the earth is sandwiched by heaven and hell. The earth is the location for the supernatural action of God and the angels, and Satan and his legions. With the coming of the Son of God from heaven and his defeat of the forces of evil, the end of time is imminent. Soon he will return on the clouds to execute God's final judgement upon the living and the dead.

This is judged a mythological outlook by Bultmann insofar as it conceptualizes the transcendent and other-worldly in terms of the immanent and this-worldly. It attempts to depict non-objective realities in terms of objective categories, and in doing so it must be criticized as scientifically false and theologically inappropriate.

Demythologizing seeks to bring out the real intention of myth, namely, its intention to talk about human existence as grounded in and limited by a transcendent, unworldly power, which is not visible to objectifying thinking.[7]

It is apparent from statements like this that Bultmann's understanding of myth is set within the framework of his own theological position. Its relation to 'objectifying' patterns of thought is crucial to his insistence that myth is inappropriate scientifically *and* theologically. The need for the translation of myth into existential categories is therefore entirely consistent with his theology prior to 1941. This identification of myth with objectivizing patterns of thought in theology also helps to explain the extensive scope of the demythologizing programme. The category of myth includes not only primitive Jewish eschatological concepts but dogmatic theories of the incarnation, the atonement, the resurrection and the Trinity. Once we realize the extent to which myth embraces all objectivizing formulations we shall cease to be surprised at Bultmann's claim that so much of the New Testament is mythological.

It is not entirely clear when Bultmann first encountered the slogan 'demythologizing' and made the connection between myth and objectivizing patterns of thought in theology. It may well have been through a 1928 dissertation on St Augustine by his pupil Hans Jonas, although this has been confirmed neither by Jonas nor by Bultmann himself. It is clear however that the eventual use of the slogan was fully compatible with his earlier hermeneutical and theological convictions.[8]

The mythical outlook of the New Testament is untenable because it is at odds with the inescapable world-view of modern science. Today the events that occur within this world are to be explained by reference to natural forces and not by supernatural agencies. The frequent intervention of angels and demons as the explanation of a wide variety of phenomena is no longer an option for the twentieth-century believer. The universe, as we know it, is much vaster than the ancients believed, and is under the regular sway of natural laws. Everything from the movement of the planets to the sickness of human beings is to be explained scientifically rather than supernaturally.

> We cannot use electric lights and radios and, in the event of illness, avail ourselves of modern medical and clinical means and at the same time believe in the spirit and wonder world of the New Testament.[9]

Bultmann refers repeatedly to the closed continuum of cause and effect which constitutes our natural world. The traditional idea of miracle is no longer part of our intellectual furniture (not at any rate if we are consistent).[10] God is not to be found repeatedly intervening in this continuum. Scientists and historians no longer have recourse to theological hypotheses for explaining natural phenomena. Even when it is recognized that, at a subatomic level, events possess a certain randomness, there is no question of returning to a world-view in which God is posited as a causal agency between events.[11] The quantum physicist is not about to rehabilitate the old mytho-logical outlook.

Insofar as there is a strong critical streak running through the demythologizing programme, Bultmann's indebtedness to the lib-eral tradition is apparent. In his sense of distance from the world-view of the New Testament he reflects the influence of teachers like Weiss and Bousset, whose work constantly emphasized the way in which the New Testament was embedded in the strange thought-world of the first century. Bultmann's demythologizing work is a deliberate recall of this emphasis as a corrective against increasingly reactionary tendencies in theology.

> If for the last twenty years we have been called back from cri-ticism to simple acceptance of the New Testament kerygma, theology and the church have run the risk of uncritically repristi-nating New Testament mythology, thereby making the kerygma unintelligible for the present. The critical work of earlier genera-tions cannot be simply thrown away but must be positively appropriated. If this does not happen, sooner or later—provided church and theology continue to exist at all— the old battles between orthodoxy and liberalism will have to be fought all over again.[12]

New Testament myth, however, is not merely to be eliminated. Here Bultmann is critical of many of his liberal teachers. Myth must be interpreted in order to expose the theological truth that it enshrines. The proclamation of the New Testament presents a new understanding of human existence in which God is apprehended personally rather than in a pseudo-scientific manner. When this proclamation is existentially interpreted its true character becomes apparent. To tie Christian faith to the intellectual acceptance of a particular world-view is to misconstrue its character. This would amount to nothing more than a search for false security, which substitutes for the trust demanded of the believer. (In this con-nection Bultmann appeals repeatedly to the work of his teacher, Wilhelm Herrmann, and in doing so demonstrates again the forma-tive influence of Herrmann's theology.)

The mythological categories of the New Testament must be

translated into existential language. Accordingly, Bultmann appeals once more to the understanding of human existence outside faith and the understanding of human existence under faith as the categories into which New Testament myth is to be translated. The besetting human condition of searching in vain for self-justification and security is overcome by the forgiveness and freedom that one finds upon hearing and receiving the word of God. This word is the proclamation of the cross of Christ as the event by which God establishes our new existential possibility.

Bultmann is here arguing that God is not revealed in a way that is accessible to the scientific or historical observer but is only disclosed in the life of the individual person. God's revelatory activity thus takes the form of personal address. If we were to suggest that Bultmann is contradicting himself by reintroducing the idea of God's invasion of the natural continuum of cause and effect, he would reply that the action of God is not to be located as an objective phenomenon occurring *between* the events of this world. The action of God occurs *within* the events of history and can only be apprehended by an act of personal discernment. It seems that for Bultmann an event can have both a scientific explanation and a theological meaning. He refers to the 'paradoxical identity' of world occurrence and divine action in which an ordinary event with a natural explanation can be the vehicle for God's revelation.

> In faith I can understand an event occurring to me as God's gift or judgment, although I can also view it within its natural or historical context. In faith I can also understand a thought or a decision as effected by God without thereby tearing it out of the continuum of its innerworldly motivation.[13]

This revelation, however, can only be known in an appropriate manner, i.e. existentially. The central instance of this is the crucifixion of Jesus of Nazareth. To the historian this is simply another world occurrence with an historical explanation. Yet for the believer it becomes God's eschatological action as it is acknowledged in personal faith. The notion of the action of God in Jesus Christ is perceived by Bultmann to be an integral feature of the kerygma rather than part of the mythological baggage which needs to be discarded.

> As the salvation occurrence, then, the cross of Christ is not a mythical event but a historical occurrence (*ein geschichtliches*

Geschehen) that has its origin in the historical event of the crucifixion of Jesus of Nazareth (*dem historischen Ereignis*).[14]

This concentration upon the cross of Christ as the event by which a new mode of existence becomes possible is already evident in the writings of Paul and John. Paul asserts that the turning point from the old world to the new has taken place in Jesus Christ, and the fourth gospel presents the Christ event even more radically as the eschatological occurrence. Insofar as the demythologizing of the traditional eschatology has already been begun here, we may say that the New Testament itself invites us to demythologize its contents.

It may be argued, however, that in the New Testament the proclamation of the crucifixion cannot be detached from the proclamation of the resurrection. Is Bultmann intent on demythologizing the former but not the latter? Bultmann agrees that cross and resurrection have to be held together; we see this most clearly in the fourth gospel where the glorification and exaltation of Jesus coincide with his being lifted up on the cross. But it is for this very reason that the resurrection cannot be seen as a separate, datable event alongside the crucifixion. There is undoubtedly a tendency in the New Testament to treat the resurrection as the resuscitation of Jesus' corpse thirty-six hours after his death. But the reports of the empty tomb must be seen as legendary, claims Bultmann, and in any event they cannot verify the truth of the Christian faith. The resurrection as the eschatological event is itself an object of faith and cannot, therefore, supply external support for faith.

For Bultmann, the resurrection as an eschatological occurrence can only refer to the significance of the crucifixion and the miracle of faith in which it is perceived. The empty tomb and the appearances of Jesus are neither necessary nor relevant to this. The resurrection is better understood as an event for the believer rather than an event for Jesus. We might describe Bultmann's understanding of the resurrection as an event in which the existential meaning of the crucifixion is experienced.

> The event of Easter, insofar as it can be referred to as a historical event (*historisches Ereignis*) alongside of the cross, is nothing other than the emergence of faith in the risen one in which the proclamation has its origin.[15]

Bultmann's interpretation of the resurrection provides us with a perfect example of the nature of his demythologizing programme.

His historical scepticism and intellectual liberalism tell us that the resurrection cannot be understood as the literal rising of a dead man from his tomb. At the same time his theological convictions insist that faith is not to be verified in this way. To seek such support for faith is to misunderstand it. The resurrection must be seen as a way of expressing the significance of the cross of Christ as the eschatological event. As I take up the cross in faith, Christ becomes risen in my life. This is an action of God but it is not one that is apparent to historical investigation. It is known only existentially in the moment of faith.

If the critic asks how faith is to be validated Bultmann will dismiss this as a pseudo-question. The witness of faith is not to be verified by historical investigation into the circumstances of Jesus' rising from the dead. To ask for proof is to evade the need for existential decision. The only way to understand the proclamation is to believe it. It is within the circle of faith alone that the witness of the Church can be perceived.[16] Bultmann is even willing to speak about the demythologizing programme as the epistemological parallel to the doctrine of justification by faith alone, and to echo Luther's language about entering into the inner darkness.

> In point of fact, radical demythologizing is the parallel to the Pauline–Lutheran doctrine of justification through faith alone without the works of the law. Or, rather, it is the consistent application of this doctrine to the field of knowledge. Like the doctrine of justification, it destroys every false security and every false demand for security, whether it is grounded on our good action or on our certain knowledge.[17]

Myth, God and the cross

Seldom has a single theological essay provoked such controversy as 'Neues Testament und Mythologie'. Even during the war years it aroused a conservative backlash amongst Bultmann's colleagues in the Confessing Church. In 1942 a convention of Berlin pastors denounced the essay in terms which branded it as heretical. Yet there were always those who were willing to speak in favour of Bultmann. Dietrich Bonhoeffer declared the statement of the Berlin convention to be a disgrace for the Confessing Church, and he spoke warmly of Bultmann's intellectual honesty and of the breath of fresh air that his work had brought.[18]

In the years after 1945 the demythologizing controversy was to gather momentum, particularly in Germany where it engulfed both the theological faculties and the churches. A measure of the consternation that Bultmann's work had caused came in a pronouncement, by the bishops of the United Evangelical-Lutheran Church, which was read from pulpits across Germany in the Sunday before Advent, 1953.

In recent years a new anxiety has arisen within the Church, and with good reason. Some theologians in our universities, eager to find new ways to commend the gospel message to the modern world, have set about 'demythologizing' the New Testament, as they call it. In so doing, they are in danger of reducing parts of the New Tastament, and even of abandoning it altogether. They rightly perceive that the New Testament is couched in the language and thought forms of the age in which it was written. But we are bound to ask whether this movement is not leading to a denial of the facts to which Scripture bears witness.[19]

This instruction was a thinly disguised attack upon the work of Bultmann. Others rallied to his support and an intense debate was waged throughout the 1950s. Many of the more notable contributions were published in *Kerygma und Mythos* which ran to numerous volumes and eventually became an international forum for discussing Bultmann's programme. In England during the 1960s, Bultmann's name was prominent in the *Honest to God* controversy, and he himself made a sympathetic contribution to the debate.[20] Under the impact of criticism, Bultmann attempted to defend and clarify his own position. While the discussion threatened to become turgid and repetitive, it is possible to identify the more perceptive criticisms, many from Swiss thinkers, that were levelled against Bultmann, and to consider the development of his position in response.

The claim was made by both philosophers and theologians that the attempt to remove all mythological elements from the Christian proclamation was ultimately reductionist. Karl Jaspers argued that the myth and the message were inseparable for any religious outlook. The transcendental dimension of human experience can only be articulated through the medium of myth. While myths have their limitations and their dangers they cannot be discarded. They are necessary ciphers for evoking an awareness of the deepest realities in human experience.

The real task, therefore, is not to demythologize, but to recover mythical thought in its original purity, and to appropriate, in this form of thinking, the marvellous mythical contents that deepen us morally, enlarge us as human beings, and indirectly bring us closer to the lofty, imageless transcendence, the idea of God which no myth can fully express for it surpasses them all.[21]

For Jaspers, the myths of the resurrection and the incarnation are essential to what the Christian faith has to say about the ultimate reality behind all things. From a more traditional theological perspective, Emil Brunner argued that myth was a vital feature of the kerygma. It had to be distinguished from the biblical world-view and, unlike the latter, preserved. The revelation of God in history demanded that God be spoken of in personal terms. The language that the New Testament employs to describe the person and work of Christ may be mythical but it remains an adequate and indispensable witness.[22]

Bultmann's response to these attempts to retain a mythological element in our religious language was to argue that they did not reckon seriously enough with the manner in which myth seeks to objectify what by its very nature cannot be objectified. The reality of God can only be apprehended existentially and not by framing 'objective' pictures of God's being and action. The nature of God demands that myths be subject to an interpretation which purges them of their naive conceptuality. Rather than destroying the reality of God, demythologizing seeks to be faithful to it.[23]

This response immediately raises a further question. If God cannot be spoken of mythologically then how else are we to speak of God? What language is available to the theologian which does not simply reduce God-talk to human self-description? Bultmann's rather surprising rejoinder is to appeal to a doctrine of analogy. We can speak of God analogically, as a person who addresses and confronts us and is disposed towards us in a particular way.

God's love and care, etc., are not images or symbols; these conceptions mean real experiences of God as acting here and now. Especially in the conception of God as Father the mythological sense vanished long ago. We can understand the meaning of the term Father as applied to God by considering what it means when we speak to our fathers or when our children speak to us as their fathers. As applied to God the physical import of the term father has disappeared completely; it expresses a purely personal relationship. It is in this analogical sense that we speak of God as Father.[24]

This sudden, unheralded appearance of a theory of analogy raises a number of difficulties. In what way is analogical language free from the objective character of mythological language? Is it possible to speak of God only relationally without at the same time committing ourselves to statements about the being of God? These questions, to which we shall return in the concluding chapter, point to a central difficulty in Bultmann's thought. How can existential interpretation avoid reducing theology to anthropology?

Another recurring criticism of Bultmann concerns his understanding of the crucifixion of Jesus. It is argued that his theology of the cross sits uneasily within his demythologizing programme and requires revision. This is a criticism which can take either of two forms. On the one hand, it can assert that Bultmann's claim that human salvation is causally dependent upon the cross is simply the last residue of mythological thought. In a consistent execution of the demythologizing programme the exclusive insistence upon the 'that' of the cross would have to be eliminated. The insistence that authentic existence is possible only through a single event occurring two thousand years ago is itself part of an archaic mythology. Thus Fritz Buri maintains:

> The assertion of a historical yet unrecognizable eschatological event in the deliverance of the Word is only a last substitute for the rejected salvation event proclaimed by the New Testament. The kerygma is a last remnant of an inconsistent yet retained mythology.[25]

This is a criticism which has been felt with increasing force in an age of religious pluralism. Where there are diverse and often competing witnesses to divine revelation it seems, to many thinkers, impossibly provincial to maintain that one event embedded within a particular tradition is the sole route to authentic existence. We shall return to this criticism also in the concluding chapter. But for the moment, we should note how Bultmann's response to this critique reveals both his Lutheranism and his continuing commitment to dialectical theology. The genuine offence of the Christian faith lies in its claim that the freedom and joy of authentic existence rest upon the grace of God given through 'Christ crucified, a stumbling block to Jews and folly to Greeks' (1 Cor 1:23). If his critics stumble upon his theology of the cross then this is nothing more and nothing less than the scandal of the Christian faith. If it is at this point that others are dismayed by his theology then he can rest content in the knowledge that what has provoked this dismay belongs to the essence of the Christian gospel. 'The purpose of demythologizing is to make the stumbling block real.'[26]

On the other hand, Bultmann's theology of the cross is criticized by those who favour a more traditional approach. Here it is maintained that more needs to be said about the death of Jesus if Bultmann's position is to be upheld. If salvation is made possible through the crucifixion of Jesus Christ, then we must be able to speak of this event in terms which express its cosmic significance. Bultmann, however, has deprived himself of these terms by the relentless pursuit of his programme. What requires revision is not his belief in the significance of the cross but his treatment of myth in the New Testament. The dependence of authentic existence upon the crucifixion cannot make sense except on the basis of a richer understanding of that event.

Eduard Schweizer has argued that the New Testament throughout focuses upon the life and death of Jesus as an episode which is of intrinsic significance and which makes Christian existence possible. The nature of this dependence is made intelligible by describing the significance of the cross in categories of sacrifice (*Opfer*) and vicarious representation (*Stellvertretung*). It is hard, he claims, to see how the cross can be understood as the event through which the world is redeemed if one cannot speak of it in these terms.[27] In a similar vein, Karl Barth maintains that the Christian life is dependent upon an event that happened once for all (*ephapax*). The nature of the Christian life can only be expressed when one has first spoken of that event in its own terms and grasped its uniqueness prior to any human response.

> [I]t seems to me that the New Testament describes the cross of Christ as an event with an inherent significance of its own. It is just because it has this inherent significance that it can become significant in the kerygma and for the faith of its recipients. I am disturbed by the way Bultmann reverses the sequence of events.[28]

In the face of this criticism, Bultmann returns to his typical claim that this is only to manifest an objectifying pattern of thought. The position of both Schweizer and Barth suggests that one can first survey the cross to appreciate its meaning and then grasp it in faith. This is to objectify what must be understood existentially. It is only in relational categories that the nature of faith in the cross is articulated. To construct a theory of the atonement in terms of vicarious sacrifice or penal substitution is to transpose the existential truth into an inappropriate subject–object pattern of thought. Thus he writes in a letter to Barth:

I can see well enough that in the NT the cross of Christ is described as an *intrinsically* significant event which *then* may and can become significant for faith too. But I cannot follow this sequence which is possible in mythological thinking, because I cannot understand the phrase 'intrinsically' significant; I can understand significance only as a relation.[29]

Barth continues the exchange:

It seems to me that we are like a whale (do you know Melville's remarkable book *Moby Dick*? You ought to have a high regard for it because of its animal mythology!) and an elephant meeting with boundless astonishment on some oceanic shore. It is all for nothing that the one sends his spout of water high in the air. It is all for nothing that the other moves its trunk now in friendship and now in threat. They do not have a common key to what each would obviously like to say to the other in its own speech and in terms of its own element.[30]

Theological method

This playful image indicates the impasse that arose between Bultmann and his critics in the demythologizing controversy. The impasse was created by the radical nature of Bultmann's polemic against objectifying patterns of thought in theology. Time and again when criticisms were levelled against him Bultmann would remain unmoved, remarking merely that his opponents were still in the grip of mythological thinking and had not appreciated the content of his hermeneutical proposals.

At the point of dialogical breakdown between Barth and Bultmann we encounter fundamentally different theological methods (despite many material similarities). While for Barth the past events of Christ's life and death possess their own unique significance, for Bultmann this significance can only be known as it is encountered in the present. At the root of this disagreement there are rival understandings of the relation of subject and object in knowledge, the meaning of revelation, and the nature of time. For Bultmann, the subject–object pattern of thought must be banished in a proper understanding of the historicity of human existence. For Barth, by contrast, the nature of God's revelation in Christ is such that its objectivity must be stressed and this may entail retaining subject–object forms of expression. For Bultmann, God's revelation occurs in the event of its appropriation and cannot find expression independently of this existential moment. For Barth, the time of Jesus Christ is determinative of all time and is therefore the locus of meaning for human existence everywhere.[31]

The roots of demythologizing lie in Bultmann's fundamental theological method. His lifelong polemic against theologies which reduce faith to a world-view, and his perpetual insistence upon the historicity of human existence find expression in the demythologizing programme. It is for this reason that his essays on demythologizing must be read alongside his other writings on hermeneutics and theological method. By studying various companion writings we can avoid the error of seeing Bultmann's programme as a purely reductionist enterprise.

The essay 'Theology as science' was delivered as a lecture in 1941 at a gathering of pastors belonging to the Confessing Church. It remained unpublished until 1984, the centenary of his birth,[32] but it reveals the extent to which a clear and positive conception of the theological task governs the writings on demythologizing. In many ways the ideas presented here were developed by Bultmann in his lectures on '*Theologische Enzyklopädie*' from 1926 to 1936. These too remained unpublished until 1984.[33]

The scientific character of theology is apparent in the way in which theology has its own proper object of study to which it seeks to be faithful. In this pursuit theology cannot adopt the procedure of the natural sciences in which the investigator stands over against the object of enquiry in a manner of relative detachment. (It must be pointed out that it is not clear how well this describes natural science in a quantum age). The natural scientist seeks to understand the object in terms of its inner structure. In this respect, science is a disinterested activity insofar as it is not immediately connected with any practical purpose or interest. Doubtless science is deeply connected with practical pursuits, but the truth of its hypotheses is not determined by criteria of utility. In theology, by contrast, there can be no commensurate detachment or neutrality.[34]

The procedure of natural science is inappropriate to the most fundamental questions of human existence. The human being is an historical individual whose existence is free and undetermined. I cannot understand myself by prescinding from the conditions of historical existence. To analyse human beings as a zoologist might study a species is inevitably to distort the nature of my existence. The same applies to the study of God. The reality of God is an all-encompassing reality which determines every facet and moment of my existence. The mode of knowledge that is appropriate to the nature of God is an historical, existential mode. The knowledge of God is only possible on the basis of God's revelation, and the form that this knowledge takes is faith.

> God is no longer God if he is thought of as an object that stands outside of thought and over against it. Unless we think of God in a proper sense, as the All-powerful who completely determines our existence, then we have not thought of him at all.[35]

God is thus not an object at our disposal. There is no timeless or detached theological truth which is available independently of faith. God is known only on the basis of God's personal address in the here and now of existence, and, therefore, theology must be a movement of faith in which faith seeks to understand itself.[36]

Bultmann's polemic against objectifying methods of thought does not render theology a purely subjective and arbitrary pursuit. It is in order to be faithful to the object of theology, namely God, that the existential mode of theological knowledge is insisted upon. In this sense, theology remains as scientific and as objective as any other discipline.[37] The theologian is as passionately concerned with truth as is any other scientific investigator. Theological truth does not depend upon the constructions and decisions of each individual; it resides in the action of God and the relationship of everything else to God. In this respect there is a strong realist streak in Bultmann's theology. Truth is not created by the decisions and commitments of the individual believer. The universal truth of God's action in Christ is discovered by the person who apprehends it in faith, or, perhaps we should say, is apprehended by it in faith.[38]

For Bultmann the form and content of theological knowledge can never be divorced. The object of faith, *fides quae creditur*, can never be understood in detachment from the act of faith, *fides qua creditur*. The error of liberal theology is to concentrate on the act of faith as a phenomenon to be analysed whereas the corresponding error of orthodoxy is to perceive faith as a doctrinal deposit which can be taught and transmitted.[39] In both cases, the act and the object of knowledge are sundered. Faith is a knowledge of God's acting upon one, and since we have no other access to God, the content and the character of faith can never be separated. As Herrmann taught, the ground and the object of faith are identical. This entails that we have only a knowledge of God's action upon us, and never of God's innermost being.

It is on the basis of this conception of the nature of theology that Bultmann's handling of the cross must be understood. To speak of the intrinsic significance of that event in a way that fails to make mention of the character of faith is to distort its meaning. The emphasis, in Bultmann's theology, must always fall upon the present as the revelatory moment in which God's action is perceived. It is only as the recurring eschatological occurrence that the significance of the crucifixion is realized.

> In the proclaiming word and in the faith that is open to this word, God's act in Christ continues to take place, and, therefore, is precisely not a past historical event under whose impact we still live but rather is the 'eschatological' occurrence. It is visible only to the very faith to which it itself occurs. Faith is not taking notice of an event of the past that is mediated by historical tradition but rather itself belongs to the eschatological occurrence by virtue of the proclamation in which this occurrence continues to take place.[40]

It becomes clear therefore that the dispute over the theology of the cross must be understood in the light of Bultmann's fundamental theological method. If the critic wishes to present an alternative theology of the cross, then Bultmann's basic theological presuppositions must first be contested. We shall return to this in the final chapter.

Miracle and divine action

One further area of conflict in the demythologizing controversy concerns Bultmann's rejection of miracle and his insistence that the natural world is a closed causal continuum. It could be argued that here he is in fact misrepresenting modern science, for the closed web of causality is not a scientific axiom which excludes the possibility of miracle. The scientist does not make the assumption that God cannot intervene in the course of nature. The only assumption the scientist makes is that, in the search for the natural explanations of types of event, considerations of divine intervention are largely irrelevant. This resembles more a working assumption about the proper domain of natural science than a philosophical conviction about the impossibility of miracles.

In this connection, Bultmann fails to take sufficient notice of human agency. In the purposive action of responsible agents we encounter many times each day breaches in the natural continuum of cause and effect. The causes of change in the natural world are often to be ascribed to human intelligence, purpose and will. My intentions and character are irrevocably bound up with the way I act in the public, observable world. Bultmann's tendency to overlook this reflects his rather Kantian isolation of the self from the social and natural world. He cannot be wholly correct when he states,

> The love of another person encounters me and is what it is only as event; it cannot be perceived as love by an objectifying view but only by me myself as the one affected by it.[41]

The love of one person for another may be perfectly apparent to me through a perception of words and deeds in the public world. There is no doubt that my discernment will be conditioned by my own understanding and experience, but to disjoin public and private perception so radically is to distort the way the world is. To conceal the true self of the agent behind the façade of public action, and to make communication only possible in some mysterious existential encounter, is to distort the human situation. My true identity cannot be filtered out from my embodied existence in the social world.

This creates a theological problem when the action of God is considered. According to Bultmann, the action of God is to be perceived not between observable events but only in and through them. This however would seem to put the action of God in a constant relation to every single natural event. If there is a paradoxical identity between divine action and natural causation then the only thing that makes one event more revelatory than another is the perception of the human subject. Bultmann seems to set up a dualism between God and the world in which the action of God can be discerned behind everything that happens, without actually interfering in it.

To be defended, Bultmann's theology of the cross seems to

demand a stronger account of divine action. If the will of God is to be discerned supremely in one historical episode, then the activity of God must here be more direct for this perception to be valid. The God who addresses and encounters us in Jesus of Nazareth must be capable of acting *upon* history rather than merely *within* it. Thus Hans Jonas:

> What is here talked about if not an *irruption* of transcendence into immanence? Those who experienced and spoke thus were not discoverers of a hidden God, but hearers of a God *making himself* known and *willing*, through them, to make himself known to all the world. The initiative is his, and that presupposes a *will* on the part of Him who reveals himself and *power* to do so, that is, to act *into* the world, and this via the human soul. I repeat: 'into' the world and by particular act, not simply 'in' the world and by way of its everpresent fitness for a transcendent interpretation.[42]

Perhaps the most serious difficulty facing a theory of divine action concerns not the rise of modern science but the ancient problem of human suffering. This receives surprisingly little direct treatment in Bultmann's work. If the world is susceptible to occasional divine intervention, then the problem of why divine action seems so infrequent and arbitrary becomes acutely felt. If God can and does intervene in the chain of natural events, why does this not happen more often in order to offset the worst effects of human malevolence and natural misfortune? This is surely the most serious problem facing an account of God's action and it is in the face of this issue that the theology of the cross must be forged.[43]

Notes

1   Schubert Ogden in Preface, NTM, p. vii.

2   *Neues Testament und Mythologie* (1941). The most recent edition was published in 1988 by Chr. Kaiser, Munich, and contains a helpful introduction from Eberhard Jüngel outlining the historical setting of the essay. 'The New Testament and mythology', NTM, pp. 1–43.

3   Cited by Antje Bultmann Lemke, 'Der unveröffentliche Nachlass von Rudolf Bultmann' in B. Jaspert (ed.), *Rudolf Bultmanns Werk und Wirkung* (Darmstadt, 1984), p. 204.

4   'Die Frage der natürlichen Offenbarung' originally appeared with

'Neues Testament und Mythologie' in *Offenbarung und Heils-geschehen* (BEvTh, Band 7, Munich, 1941); 'The question of natural revelation', EPT, pp. 90–118.

5   EPT, pp. 105–6.

6   Cf. W. Schmithals, *An Introduction to the Theology of Rudolf Bultmann* (London, 1968), pp. 249ff.

7   'Zum Problem der Entmythologisierung' (1952); 'On the problem of demythologizing', NTM, p. 99.

8   For a discussion of the origins of the term 'demythologizing' see Roger Johnson, *The Origins of Demythologizing* (Leiden, 1974), pp. 96ff.; J.M. Robinson, 'The pre-history of demythologization', *Interpretation* 20 (1966), pp. 65–77; John Painter, *Theology as Hermeneutics* (Sheffield, 1987), pp. 134–44.

9   'New Testament and mythology', NTM, p. 4.

10 'On the problem of demythologizing', NTM, p. 96.

11 JCM, p. 15.

12 'New Testament and mythology', NTM, pp. 11–12.

13 'On the problem of demythologizing', NTM, pp. 111ff.; cf. JCM, pp. 62ff.

14 'New Testament and mythology', NTM, p. 35.

15 Ibid., p. 39.

16 Ibid.

17 'On the problem of demythologizing', NTM, p. 122.

18 Eberhard Bethge, *Dietrich Bonhoeffer* (London, 1970), p. 616; cf. Gerhard Krause, 'Dietrich Bonhoeffer and Rudolf Bultmann' in James Robinson (ed.), *The Future of our Religious Past* (London, 1971), pp. 279–305.

19 Cited by Hans-Werner Bartsch, 'The present state of the debate', K & M II, pp. 1–2. In 1974 the Lutheran Bishops Conference officially expressed their regret to Bultmann personally for this earlier pronouncement. Cf. Eduard Lohse, 'Die Evangelische Kirche vor der Theologie Rudolf Bultmanns', *Zeitschrift für Theologie und Kirche* 82 (1985), pp. 173–91.

20 J.A.T. Robinson, *Honest to God* (London, 1963); 'Bultmann' in J.A.T. Robinson and D.L. Edwards (eds), *The Honest to God Debate* (London, 1965), pp. 134–8.

21 Karl Jaspers, 'Myth and religion', K & M II, pp. 145–6.

22 E. Brunner, *The Christian Doctrine of Creation and Redemption* (London, 1952), pp. 268ff.

23 Cf. Bultmann's response to Jaspers, 'Antwort an Karl Jaspers' (1954); 'The case for demythologizing', K & M II, p. 193. The complete

exchange between Bultmann and Jaspers is published in *Die Frage der Entmythologisierung* (Munich, 1954). It is discussed by A. Malet in *The Thought of Rudolf Bultmann* (Shannon, 1969), pp. 337–75.

24 JCM, p. 69. In defence of these remarks Bultmann appeals to Erich Frank's *Philosophical Understanding and Religious Truth* (New York, 1945), pp. 161ff., where an approach to an existentialist doctrine of analogy is outlined. Yet the relevance of Frank's work for Bultmann's theology is not entirely apparent since Frank does not appear to adopt Bultmann's wholesale critique of mythological and objectifying patterns of thought. Cf. John Macquarrie, 'Bultmann's understanding of God' in *Thinking About God* (London, 1975), p. 183.

25 'Entmythologisierung oder Entkerygmatisierung der Theologie', KuM II, p. 96.

26 'The case for demythologizing', K & M II, p. 193.

27 'Zur Interpretation des Kreuzes bei R. Bultmann' in *Aux Sources de la Tradition Chrétienne* (Neuchâtel, 1950), p. 237.

28 'Rudolf Bultmann—an attempt to understand him', K & M II, pp. 98–9.

29 *Letters*, p. 93.

30 Ibid., p. 105.

31 This contrast of fundamental approaches is analysed by Friedrich Gogarten, *Demythologizing and History* (London, 1955); Heinrich Ott, 'Objectification and existentialism', K & M II, pp. 306–35; A. Malet, *The Thought of Rudolf Bultmann*, pp. 376–426.

32 'Theologie als Wissenschaft' (1941); 'Theology as science', NTM, pp. 45–67.

33 TE, ch. 3, pp. 35–65.

34 'Theology as science', NTM, pp. 45–9.

35 TE, p. 55. The translation is my own.

36 'Theology as science', NTM, p. 55.

37 Ibid., pp. 66–7.

38 Cf. 'Wissenschaft und Wahrheit', TE, pp. 35–50; For an exegesis of this conception of theology see Eberhard Jüngel, *Glauben und Verstehen* (Heidelberg, 1985), pp. 38ff.

39 'Theology as science', NTM, pp. 51ff.

40 Ibid., p. 54.

41 'On the problem of demythologizing', NTM, p. 114.

42 'Is faith still possible? Memories of Rudolf Bultmann and reflections on the philosophical aspects of his work', *Harvard Theological Review* 75 (1982), p. 20.

43 Cf. Jürgen Moltmann, *The Crucified God* (London, 1974), esp. ch. 6, pp. 200–90.

7

Post-Bultmannian Perspectives

In the course of this study, we have had occasion to consider recurrent criticisms that have been levelled against Bultmann. In this concluding chapter, we shall reconsider four of these criticisms which represent, to a large extent, the theological agenda in the post-Bultmannian era. We shall discover that while there is something like a consensus on the weaknesses of Bultmann's theology, there is no general agreement as to what direction a more satisfactory alternative might lie in. This, in itself, is a comment on the fragmented state of contemporary Christian theology.

Objectivity and theological language

Bultmann's relentless hostility to objectivizing patterns of thought in theology is apparent both in the early essays of the 1920s, and in the demythologizing debate which dominated the later part of his career. In order to safeguard the transcendence of God and the existential character of faith, Bultmann repeatedly resists any manoeuvre which will objectify the reality of God. This criticism applies both to liberal theology and to the return to dogmatics in the theology of Karl Barth.

Bultmann is adamant that his eschewal of objectivizing modes of thought and speech does not result in the reduction of faith to a purely subjective phenomenon. On the contrary, his resolute refusal of objectivity is designed to prevent faith becoming reduced to a human work; it is a defence of the truly objective character of theological science. According to his critics, however, this will not work in the way Bultmann intends.

A central weakness in his theology concerns the nature of religious language. It is no accident that he lacks an adequate theory of religious language (other than the rather belated appeal to the need for a doctrine of analogy), since this is a direct corollary of his theological epistemology. By his persistent rejection of anything that could be construed as an objectifying move in theology, he has declared any adequate theory of religious language illegitimate. We simply have recourse to the language of existential encounter and, despite Bultmann's assurances to the contrary, it is unclear how he can prevent theological language becoming reduced to a logically proper idiom of human self-description.

This uneasiness about the lack of a proper understanding of religious language is reflected in several lines of criticism. For instance, Karl Barth's protest against Bultmann's demythologizing programme can be read as a defence of the unalterable *objectivity* of God's revelation in Jesus Christ. It is by virtue of the priority of the events of revelation, which are significant in themselves, that the existence of the Christian is determined. This demands our witness to the objectivity of Christ incarnate, crucified and risen.

> The major affirmations of the creed . . . define the being and action of the God who is different from man and encounters man; the Father, the Son and the Holy Ghost. For this reason alone they cannot be reduced to statements about the inner life of man. . . . The anthropological strait-jacket into which Bultmann forces his systematic theology, and unfortunately his exegetical theology as well, represents a tradition which goes back to W. Herrmann and even further to Ritschl and Schleiermacher.[1]

According to Barth, the language of Christian confession is determined by the objectivity of God's revelation. The fundamental character of theological speech is therefore that of 'witness'. It is not primarily to their own existence or self-understanding that believers must refer, but, first and foremost, to Jesus Christ as he is spoken of in the Scriptures.

> [T]he language of the prophets and apostles about God's revelation is not a free, selective and decisive treatment of well-found convictions, but—which is something different—witness. That is, it is an answer to what is spoken to them, and an account of what is heard by them. That is why their order of knowing

127

corresponds to the order of being in which God is the Lord but in which man is God's creature and servant. That is why their thought and language follow the fact of God's revelation, freely created and provided by Him.[2]

The nature of revelation, and hence the proper subject matter of theology, demands that we recognize its objectivity. This is not a return to the objectivity which Bultmann claimed could only represent a dry and sterile orthodoxy of the intellect. According to Barth, it is an objectivity which has an accompanying subjectivity in the work of the Holy Spirit.[3] It is only through the illuminating work of the Spirit upon believers in their own time and situation that the objectivity of revelation is recognized. Thus the witness of the Christian is itself an act dependent upon and compelled by the Holy Spirit. To this extent, Barth will claim that his own theology acknowledges the existential and actualist character of our knowledge of God. This aspect, however, can only be grasped where there is a logically prior acknowledgement of the objectivity of revelation in Jesus Christ. The peculiarity of Christian faith is that it is directed towards an objective basis in a manner that is totally self-involving.[4]

The confession of faith is itself made possible by its object, namely God. According to Barth, it is the activity of God which creates a correspondence between human speech and divine revelation. Human confession cannot capture the glory and mystery of God's being but it does bear an analogical relation to it, not by virtue of an innate human capacity but through the power of the word of God. Barth thus sets up a doctrine of analogy which delineates the manner in which it is possible for the human subject to speak of the being and action of God. He describes this as an analogy of faith (*analogia fidei*) in order to emphasize its dependence upon the activity of God who is both its object and creator.[5]

In order to clarify the Church's proclamation of the revelation of God that is attested in Scripture, theologians must place at the forefront of all their speaking about God the doctrine of the Trinity.

The doctrine of the Trinity is what basically distinguishes the Christian concept of revelation as Christian, in contrast to all other possible doctrines of God or concepts of revelation.[6]

For Barth, unlike Bultmann, we must speak of both the being and the action of God. These cannot be separated if revelation is to be acknowledged as the self-revelation of God. The doctrine of the

Trinity must therefore inform everything that is said of the being, purposes, and action of God. Unless we learn to speak of God as Father, Son and Spirit we cannot understand the other doctrines of the faith, including those that relate to the Christian life. The existence of the believer is cast within the framework of the purpose of the triune God in creation, reconciliation and redemption. In Barth's theology, the life and work of the believer find their place within a universe of discourse which is necessary if God's self-revelation is to be perceived and appropriated. The concepts and grammar of this discourse are themselves commandeered by that same revelation, and they are the necessary vehicles for the Church's understanding of its message. Thus, we can see in Barth the different role that is played by theological speech which is determined by his belief in the irreducible objectivity of God's revelation.[7]

A related though more philosophical criticism of Bultmann's treatment of religious language is the claim, by several recent writers, that 'myth' is indispensable for the expression of truths that are embodied in a religious understanding of reality. Mircea Eliade's work is the *locus classicus* for this interpretation of myth. He argues that myths are indispensable in certain cultures for the way in which they enable communities to find meaning and value in life. The myth, through its cosmic story form, legitimizes patterns of belief and behaviour, and establishes a world of meaning in which the sacred is experienced. It is through the recitation or ritual re-enactment of the myth that it continues to have meaning and to shape the lives of its participants.[8]

Arguing on the basis of this understanding of myth, Ian Barbour has criticized Bultmann for his reduction of the mythological to the self-understanding of the human subject.[9] The demythologizing programme leads to a neglect of God's relation to nature and history, and it fails to do justice to the cognitive content of the Christian myths. According to Barbour, myths can embody analogical models which represent the being and purposes of God in relation to the created order. To jettison the myth is to run the risk of losing the conception of reality that is embodied in the religion.

> Models summarize the structural elements of a set of myths. They can represent aspects of the cosmic order, including nature and history, which are dramatized in myth but which tend to be neglected in Bultmann's de-mythologized existentialism. Like myths, models offer ways of ordering experience and of interpreting the world. They are neither literal pictures of reality nor

useful fictions. They lead to conceptually formulated, systematic, coherent, religious beliefs which can be criticaly analysed and evaluated.[10]

A further critique of Bultmann's inattention to theological language is found within the Bultmannian school, in Schubert Ogden's *Christ Without Myth*, probably the most important contribution to the demythologizing debate by an English-speaking theologian. Ogden agrees with Bultmann that all talk of God must simultaneously be talk of human existence, and that any attempt to divorce the two will lead to an outmoded world-view which will distort the nature of faith. At the same time, Ogden believes that Bultmann has invited the criticism of reducing theology to anthropology by his failure to present an adequate doctrine of analogy. Bultmann's claim, that his method of demythologizing does not destroy the objectivity of faith but instead guarantees it, cannot be upheld except by a more philosophically adequate understanding of analogy in distinction from myth.

> Until it is made clear that one can speak of God 'analogically' without also having to speak of him 'mythologically', it can hardly be expected that the demand for demythologisation will be correctly understood.[11]

For Ogden, the principal alternative to the outmoded theism of classical metaphysics is found in the neo-classical metaphysics of Charles Hartshorne's process theology. The di-polar doctrine of God that is available here is one in which the being of God cannot be detached from God's relation to the world and human existence. The existential emphasis in Bultmann's thought is thus retained, although this approach requires a revision of other aspects of Bultmann's theology. Ogden believes that these further revisions are necessary, but, for the moment, it is worth noting his appeal to process thought as the means by which Bultmann's appeal to analogy is to be rescued. In Ogden's judgement, theologians need more than the ontology of human existence borrowed from Heidegger. They need a *theological* ontology in which the conditions for meaningful speech about God are set out, since there must be a way of ascribing certain attributes to God if theology is to avoid anthropological reduction.[12]

Christology and the historical Jesus

Perhaps the most controversial feature of Bultmann's work has been his apparent disregard for the historical Jesus. As a historian, he has pursued the liberal tradition of reconstructing the life of Jesus from the sources, but, as a theologian, he believes this to be an unnecessary task. It is not the teaching of Jesus that constitutes the Christian proclamation, but the Easter message of the crucified and risen Christ. In this respect, the Christ of faith displaces the teaching of the historical Jesus in the proclamation of the Church. The word of God does not depend upon our ability to reconstruct the words and actions of Jesus from the New Testament witness. The 'that' of the cross is decisive; the 'what' and the 'how' of the events preceding it are theologically marginal. To undergird the Church's proclamation by historical proof is to mistake the character of faith as existential decision and confession.

Since the 1950s, however, this position has proved to be remarkably unstable. It has been radically qualified by a group of Bultmann's most distinguished pupils, while outside the Bultmann school the quest of the historical Jesus has continued to inform the study of Christology.

In the writings of Ernst Käsemann, Günther Bornkamm, Ernst Fuchs and Gerhard Ebeling (a group sometimes referred to as right-wing Bultmannians), we find amongst Bultmann's pupils a desire to rehabilitate the historical Jesus as a theological criterion of the Christian faith.[13] Their chief complaint against Bultmann is that he fails to do justice to the nature of Christian faith as faith in *Jesus Christ*. At the heart of the kerygma there is a reference to a historical individual; a proper name grounds the Christian faith in a particular historical episode. As such, the kerygma cannot be reduced to a timeless understanding of human existence. The name of Jesus is irreducible and immediately links the meaning and truth of the proclamation to the life of one human being. The Christian faith cannot prescind from its roots in history; it stands under the lordship of Christ, and therefore the authentic words and deeds of the historical Jesus control a proper understanding of the Church's message. To reduce the historical Jesus to the mere 'that' of the cross is unsatisfactory, and it cannot be supported by the claim that those who do otherwise are searching for a false security.

We pupils owe it to our teacher to dissent from his statement that the '*that* of the coming of Jesus' is the sole identification mark of the gospel and to refuse to accept his justification of it as defence against a 'secure' faith, even if he insists on abiding by this justification. This is the only way to prevent the premature closure both of the discussion and of our own road into the future.[14]

The most sustained critique of Bultmann at this point is found in Gerhard Ebeling's *Theology and Proclamation*. It is one of the constants of the Christian faith, he argues, that it is always characterized as faith in Jesus Christ. The name is irreducible and indispensable, and all the Christological predicates employed in Scripture and tradition refer to the bearer of this name. Through this rigid designation of an individual, the authority of Jesus is central to the logical structure of the Christian faith.[15] The fact that the eschatological categories employed by the New Testament writers are applied to Jesus compels us to ask the question 'Why?', and this leads us back to the significance of Jesus' history. At the very least, historical investigation must show that Jesus was not radically different from his portrayal by the Church. If the historian could demonstrate that Jesus had been a Zealot, then the Christian assessment of his significance would have to be amended accordingly.

The revisions proposed by Käsemann, Ebeling *et al.* can be seen as a reaction against the excessive formalism which besets Bultmann's Christology. Because of his total hostility to objectivizing patterns of thought in theology, Bultmann cannot allow that any historical information about Jesus could be relevant to faith. This would amount to a category mistake. The bare fact of Jesus' crucifixion is theologically sufficient, and Bultmann claims that this is what Paul and John are really saying. Yet this raises the deep problem of why it is this particular crucified man, and not some other, who has become the focus of the kerygma. What is it about the life and work of Jesus that gives rise to the Christian faith? Ebeling is surely right when he contends that this question, far from displacing faith, is forced upon us by its very nature. If we know only of the crucifixion it is hard to avoid the conclusion that the human Jesus is only tangentially related to the kerygma, and so has 'no more importance than that of a random and meaningless cipher'.[16]

It is Bultmann's reduction of the historical Jesus to the single event of his death that has prompted several of his critics to level the charge of docetism against him. If God has acted in a decisive way in space and time, our investigation of that action cannot discard the methods of historical science. These may not be sufficient to establish the divine action, but they are necessary to clarify the context in which this action takes place. To eschew such investigation as unnecessary is to avoid the scandal of God's involvement in human history through the 'Word become flesh'. It is ironic that a theologian so insistent upon the historicity of human existence should be accused of an incipient docetism.[17]

It is worth considering briefly the function that Bultmann's revisionary followers assign to the historical Jesus. In the so-called 'new quest', Jesus becomes something like a prototype of Christian existence, who acts as an objective criterion and constraint upon the kerygma. This emerges clearly in Käsemann's programmatic lecture of 1953 to the 'Old Marburgers'.[18] The summons to believe in God, which Jesus presents to his hearers, has a strong formal similarity to the call to faith in the later kerygma. Jesus proclaims the grace of God to sinners, both in his teaching and in his consorting with tax-collectors and other social outcasts. His demand for total obedience to God in the form of love leads to the shattering of the external demands of the law. We see this in the antitheses in the Sermon on the Mount, and in his teaching about the Sabbath and the laws concerning purification.[19] In aligning himself with the cause of the Baptist, Jesus announces the breaking in of the new age, while in the parables he speaks of the unbounded generosity of God which calls forth our obedience and sacrifice. To this extent, the words and deeds of Jesus are authoritative for the Christian community.

> Can we not simply say that, while admittedly what the historical Jesus brings with him is by no means the kerygma in its later form nor indeed the whole gospel, on the other hand his words, his works, and what happened to him do point us towards keystones of the later gospel; and to this extent can be used as criteria of this gospel by a community engaged in conflict with enthusiasts?[20]

In Bornkamm's *Jesus of Nazareth*, the major portion of the sketch of the historical Jesus concerns his message. It is in his teaching about the gift and demand of God that Jesus confronts his hearers with the words of life. In hearing Jesus' word, men and women find themselves in the presence of God, and it is this same God who is heard in the Church's later proclamation of Jesus as the crucified and exalted Lord. There is thus continuity, though not identity, between the message of Jesus and the proclamation of the Church. A similar strategy for discerning the continuity between the historical Jesus and the Christ of faith is developed by James Robinson in *A New Quest of the Historical Jesus*. Bultmann's disjunction is eradicated by asserting that the encounter between God and human beings is structurally similar in the message of Jesus and the preaching of the Church. We can discern in the words of Jesus the Christian faith *in nuce*; the encounter with God in the ministry of Jesus anticipates the encounter with God after the events of Easter. While the Easter faith cannot be reduced to the teaching of the historical Jesus, it nonetheless has its historical roots therein.[21]

It is not clear, however, what the status of this position is. On the one hand, it is not so very different from the position that Bultmann himself seems to occupy in *Jesus and the Word*. Here Bultmann points to the formal and material similarities between the teaching of Jesus and the proclamation of the Church, and he is certainly not incapable of perceiving the historical continuity at this level. His argument is that when the Church's preaching of Jesus as the crucified Lord replaces Jesus' own message of the kingdom, we cannot avoid asserting the discontinuity between the two. It is the crucified Christ who has now become the object of the Church's faith and, therefore, the words of the pre-Easter Jesus have been displaced from the kerygma. As long as the new questers continue to accept this discontinuity it is not clear that their position can be very different from that of Bultmann himself. Bultmann, in his reply to his pupils, is able to exploit this ambivalence in their position.

> The Christ of the kerygma has, as it were, displaced the historical Jesus and authoritatively addressed the hearer—every hearer. So how can we speak of an identity of Jesus' activity with the kerygma in the sense that in Jesus' word and deed the kerygma is already contained *in nuce*?[22]

On the other hand, if the new questers, having identified a weakness in Bultmann's thought, wish to advance further, they need to assert a stronger continuity between the historical Jesus and the Christ of the kerygma. There are two related problems here. One is that the concentration upon the words of Jesus, and the encounter with God that they precipitate, lead only to continuity between the *message* of Jesus and the message of the Church. Yet it has been argued that the presence of the name, Jesus Christ, at the centre of the kerygma, refers us not merely to his words but to the totality of his person and work. It is Jesus himself and not simply his words which form the theme of the gospels. If we are to assert a continuity between the historical Jesus and the Christ of faith we shall have to say more about his life and death. A second difficulty in the position is that, in the case of Käsemann at least, the central criterion employed in the search for authentic information about Jesus is the criterion of dissimilarity. Yet by its very nature, this criterion cannot provide us with information which will display the continuity between the historical Jesus and the Christ of faith. Käsemann's position retains the central features of Bultmann's Christology but tries to support it by reference to some typical examples of Jesus' teaching. The impression is created that his Christology belongs in no man's land.

> It is almost as if an essentially idealist philosophy of history were being buttressed by a kind of superimposed realist dogma.[23]

If we are to hold to the identity between the historical Jesus and the proclaimed Christ, we can do so only on the basis that the latter describes the former. It is not merely that the message of Jesus prefigures the message of the Church; it must be maintained that the message of the Church witnesses to the identity of Jesus in his life, death and resurrection. The gospels do not merely witness to the bare moment of revelation. They recount the history of the Messiah as the history of Jesus of Nazareth; they report the history of this human being as the history of the Son of God.[24] While it is only post-Easter that Jesus is recognized and proclaimed as Messiah and Son of God, the pre-Easter narrative is an essential means for recounting how this is so. The significance of the crucifixion and resurrection cannot be detached from Jesus' message of the kingdom, his actions, his faith and sense of vocation, his relations with individuals and groups, and the manner in which finally he faced his death. The Christian faith is grounded upon an understanding of who Jesus is in the unity of his life, death and resurrection, and, therefore, it must presuppose a greater continuity between the historical Jesus and the Christian kerygma than Käsemann allows.[25]

Recent Christologies, both Protestant and Catholic, suggest that the quest of the historical Jesus has never really been abandoned by theologians. In part, this reflects the desire to show the way in which the kerygma is grounded in the soil of history and, in part, it reflects a belief in the necessity and benefits provided by historical criticism of the synoptic tradition. A striking example of this is Edward

Schillebeeckx's *Jesus: An Experiment in Christology*, where, with great effort, the work of historical criticism is harnessed to the presentation of a contemporary Christology. According to Schillebeeckx, historical criticism has a dual role to play in Christology. Negatively, it must assure us that Jesus was not radically different from the way in which he has been presented by the early Church. Positively, it must lay before the believer the historical events in which faith experiences its Lord. While it cannot replace faith, historical criticism must certainly be brought to its service.

One cannot go on for ever believing in ideas, whether the idea be abstract (D. Strauss's notion of 'God become man' without Jesus) or one given existential content (such as Bultmann's *kerygma*). In that way Christianity loses its universal purport and forfeits the right to continue speaking of a final saving activity of God in history: the world comes to be regulated by an *Ideengeschichte*.[26]

A strikingly different approach to the quest of the historical Jesus is found in Schubert Ogden's theology. According to Ogden, the Christ proclaimed by the Church is the Christ who is presented in the Jesus-kerygma which underlies the gospel. Through historical critical analysis, we can uncover the earliest layer of the Jesus-tradition preserved by the Church, and we can use this as a norm for the Christian faith. Thus far, Ogden agrees with the new questers in insisting that this is necessary for a proper elucidation of the content of the kerygma. Where he differs is in his claim that the Jesus who is thus disclosed is not necessarily the historical Jesus. We have no guarantee that the individual lying behind the gospel tradition corresponds to the portrait painted of him, and in any case this is not theologically necessary. Provided that God continues to encounter men and women in the preaching of the biblical Christ, we need not worry about the historical Jesus. If the earliest portrait of Jesus awakens men and women to an authentic existence in the presence of God, we can abandon our theological concern for the quest of the historical Jesus. The Jesus of faith is the existential Jesus of the gospels and not the empirical Jesus of history.[27]

While at first this position seems breathtakingly implausible, it has a certain simplicity and coherence. What functions for the Christian faith as the normative model of human existence is undoubtedly the portrait of Jesus that we find in the gospels. This portrait is authoritative and authentic for the life of the Church, and remains so irrespective of our ability to reconstruct a life of Jesus from the sources. To show that the power of the story is independent of its historical antecedents, Ogden draws a parallel with Lincoln's Gettysburg Address with its appeal to the event of 4 July 1776. For Lincoln this event functions as the 'primal authorizing source' of American patriotism. It possesses this function irrespective of the findings of the historian. As the impulse and focal point of authentic American libertarianism and egalitarianism, it cannot be falsified by the findings of historical study. Whatever may have happened that day cannot falsify the authenticity of these moral values.

> Whatever else may in fact have happened, as empirical–historical research might be able to establish, the only thing about the event that is of interest to Lincoln or to other American patriots as such is that it is the origin of a nation so conceived and so dedicated, and hence the primal and authorizing source of their own as well as all other authentic Americanism.[28]

The same is true, *mutatis mutandis*, with respect to the Jesus proclaimed by the New Testament. As the primal authorizing source of authentic human existence, the Jesus of the gospels can retain his function for believers irrespective of historical enquiry behind the kerygma. The Christ who is preached is thus the existential Jesus as opposed to the empirical Jesus. He is the one who encounters us in the preaching of the Church, and not in the hypotheses of the historians.

A similar approach to post-Bultmannian Christology can be found in Van A. Harvey's *The Historian and the Believer*. For Harvey the picture of Jesus is a perspectival image which enables us to understand human existence in its relationship before God. The name 'Jesus of Nazareth' has four discreet meanings: the actual earthly Jesus; the historical Jesus who is the sum total of our knowledge of the earthly Jesus; the memory impression (perspectival image) of Jesus which belongs to the earliest strata of the New Testament witness; and the complete biblical Christ figure with the accretions of pre-existence, virgin birth, and ascension. It is, however, the third notion of the perspectival image that Harvey believes is indispensable to the Christian faith.[29]

There are at least three difficulties with this position. Firstly, in its sophisticated drawing of distinctions between the empirical and the existential Jesus, it imposes a framework upon the New Testament which is foreign to the intention of the writers. The power and integrity of the kerygma reside in the claim that the existential Jesus of faith is also the empirical Jesus of history. The Christian faith is faith in a historical person, rather than a portrait of human existence. A second and related problem is that, despite what Ogden says, historical study could conceivably falsify many of the claims made by the New Testament writers. In this respect, his historical analogy is somewhat disingenuous. If scientific study demonstrates that a popular conception of a historical episode is fundamentally mistaken, then this will surely weaken that popular conception. To take two examples native to my own culture: if the historian reveals that the Battle of the Boyne or the ambitions of Bonnie Prince Charlie differed sharply from their popular representations, then this will inevitably call these representations into question. The interpretation of history is crucial to the legitimacy of all religious and political causes, and the findings of the historian can be disquieting for our deepest moral and theological convictions.

The third problem that besets this Christology concerns its doctrine of God. The traditional position which asserts a continuity between the historical Jesus and the kerygmatic Christ reflects a commitment to a belief in divine action. It is because of the belief that God acted once for all in the events of Jesus' life, death and resurrection that the kerygma is so closely tied to a single historical episode. If we sever the existential from the empirical we seem to threaten the conception of divine revelation which governs the Christian faith. In this respect, Ogden's Christology requires a revised understanding of the relationship of God to the world, and the related notions of revelation and salvation. Once we perceive his further departure from Bultmann on this issue we can better appreciate his Christological position.

Salvation and the Christ event

A third controversial feature of Bultmann's theology is its apparent insistence that authentic existence is only attainable through faith in the crucified Christ. Human salvation is made possible through the occurrence of a single historical event, and it is actualized only through belief in that event. It is this claim which enables Bultmann to insist that salvation is primarily the work of God in Christ, and that genuine knowledge of God is only attainable within the community of Christian faith. Here Bultmann's Lutheranism is most apparent. It is perhaps because of the modernist trends in other sectors of his theology that many critics are surprised at this soteriological traditionalism.

We have already noted in the previous chapter the criticisms levelled by Jaspers and Buri in the demythologizing debate. According to Buri, Bultmann's insistence upon the cross of Jesus as the historically necessary condition for salvation is the last vestige of Christian mythology which cries out for reinterpretation. Jaspers raises the question of those confessing other faiths and asks what Bultmann can positively say about their existence before God. If the knowledge of God and salvation (themes which cannot be separated in Bultmann's existential theology) are restricted to faith in Christ, what are we to say about the vast majority of the human race who have lived outside the Christian tradition?

It must be admitted that Bultmann has surprisingly little to say about these issues. We might venture two reasons for this. One is that European (and especially German) theology in the mid-twentieth century was preoccupied with a particular set of problems which did not include much reference to the world religions. For example, Karl Barth's critique of religion as a function of human sinfuless was directed primarily to distortions within Christianity rather than to other religious traditions.[30] Bultmann's own interest in what constituted true religion was a formative theme in his theology, and this also was a discussion largely internal to Christian theology.[31] The conflicting truth claims of different religions were not an issue high on his agenda.

Secondly, it is not clear that Bultmann's theology has the internal resources to say very much either about the uniqueness of the Christ event or about the situation of those confessing other religions. His doctrine of the cross will not allow the theologian to express its significance in terms of incarnation or atonement as these have traditionally been conceived. Yet if the uniqueness of the cross is to be insisted upon, it is hard to understand this independently of other traditional themes dealing with the person and work of Christ. It is significant that for many theologians the breakdown of traditional dogmatic themes necessitates a revision of the claim to uniqueness for the Christ event.[32] Bultmann, in dismissing the categories of Christian dogmatics while continuing to insist upon the uniqueness of the cross, appears to be caught sitting on the fence. It is not apparent, moreover, that he can say much about other religions except perhaps, as in the case of Judaism, to assign them to the sphere of law- and works-righteousness. While he does argue that all human existence is moved, at least unconsciously, by the question of

God, his polemic against natural theology seems to prevent him from discerning any knowledge of God outside the existential act of faith in Christ. Bultmann's response to John Macquarrie on this question is worth considering.

> I do not deny that there is an understanding outside of Christian faith as to what God is and what grace is. I am convinced that Augustine's words, 'Our heart is restless until it rests in Thee', are true for all men. In all men, explicitly or implicitly, the question concerning God is a living one. The exclusiveness of the kerygma consists in the fact that it provides the answer to this question by offering the right to say 'God is my God'.[33]

The ambivalence of this response reveals the weakness in Bultmann's position. On the one hand, he wants to assert a knowledge of God and of grace common to all people. Yet, on the other hand, his position forces him to reduce this to a *question* about God which only finds its answer in the Christian faith. Consistency forces him toward the latter alternative yet leaves him with little to say about the noetic state of those outside the Christian faith.

The most sustained attempt to revise Bultmann's theology at this point is again found in the work of Ogden. He argues, in characteristically robust style, that there is a collision between two fundamental propositions in Bultmann's thought.

1. *Christian faith is to be interpreted exhaustively and without remainder as the original human possibility of authentic historical* (geschichtlich) *existence, as this is conceptualized by philosophical analysis.*

2. *Christian faith is actually realizable only because of the particular historical* (historisch) *event, Jesus of Nazareth.*[34]

Under a consistent existential interpretation, Christian faith must be freed from any necessary connection with a particular historical event. Like Buri, Ogden believes that the demythologizing programme needs to be extended to purge Bultmann's theology of the cross of its traditionalism. The significance of the New Testament's witness to Jesus is that it proclaims the universal possibility of authentic existence under the grace and demand of God's love. The portrait of Jesus is the authoritative paradigm for Christians, but this does not entail that an authentic knowledge of God's love is necessarily dependent upon him. The love of God may be known in other ways and people may live authentically in other traditions.

The doctrine of God that accompanies this Christology is the process doctrine that God is the universal and creative force of love that permeates the world, and is constantly making its presence felt to human beings. The activity of God is thus the alluring and compelling power of love that infuses the creation and awakens a response in human beings.[35]

While we do not have time to assess this interesting appropriation of process thought, it is clear that the denial of the historical necessity and soteriological uniqueness of the Christ event must be accompanied by a revision of Bultmann's doctrine of God. What is not so clear is whether Bultmann would have recognized the proper development of his own intentions in this revisionary project. Throughout much of his life, Bultmann was a dialectical theologian who insisted upon the scandal of the cross as God's intersection of human history. In the Christ event, God addresses human beings once for all, and, consequently, the divine–human encounter is forever dependent upon God's having acted in a unique and decisive way. The demythologizing programme was an attempt to underscore the nature of this encounter rather than to threaten it. This is apparent in Bultmann's response to Ogden.

> Christian faith contends that the gift of radical freedom is the gift of God's grace. And Christian faith speaks about the grace of God not as an idea but as an act of God: an act which reveals itself as grace in Jesus Christ, that is, in a historical event. This assertion cannot be proved by philosophy; indeed, it is a stumbling block, a *scandalon* for rational thinking. And therefore I must ask Ogden whether what he calls the inconsistency of my proposal is not rather the legitimate and necessary character of what the New Testament calls the stumbling block?[36]

Nevertheless, it is hard to resist the conclusion that the uniqueness of the Christ event needs to be elucidated by a more positive treatment of dogmatics than we find in Bultmann's thought. The historical necessity and soteriological finality of Jesus Christ can only be articulated by a return to many of the themes relating to the person and work of Christ that are dismissed by Bultmann. (In many ways, this is a corollary of the two previous criticisms that we have noted.) In addition, a more constructive attitude towards other religions might be attained by a development of his eschatology. Bultmann's eschatology is motivated by hope in the sovereign love of the creator

God, and this may provide a better Christian perspective from which to understand other faiths. In the theology of Moltmann, for instance, we find the concept of Christ's eschatological kingdom providing a framework for a Christian theology of other religions.[37] As Paul in Romans 9 – 11 is able to see the Jewish faith in the light of God's final purposes for all the nations of the earth, so Moltmann proposes that the contribution of other faiths should be seen in the light of God's coming kingdom which has already been anticipated in the life and work of Christ. Doubtless this position faces serious difficulties of its own, but it does provide Christian theology with the opportunity of continuing to affirm the uniqueness of Christ without blithely ignoring the existence and insights of other religious communities.

Theology and politics

Another recurrent charge against Bultmann in recent literature is that his theology reflects a private religion of the human subject. It is argued that his emphasis upon the two possibilities of self-understanding that lie at the heart of existence tends to isolate the individual from the personal and social relationships that shape human identity. The hermeneutical insistence upon these dual possibilities across time and space obscures the manner in which human life is inextricably bound up with particular historical forces. Bultmann's human self is suspiciously reminiscent of the Kantian transcendental subject whose real identity lies beyond the empirical and public world. The consequence of this is that his theology assumes an apolitical character, and thus lacks the necessary cutting edge to criticize the circumstances of the present.

A seminal statement of this criticism is found in Moltmann's *Theology of Hope,* where it is argued that Bultmann's emphasis upon the individual subject is essentially a modern phenomenon which distorts the message of the Bible. According to Moltmann, the abstraction of the human being from its relationships to other people and to the world can be traced back through Kant to the philosophy of Descartes. For Descartes, the project of pure knowledge begins with the assertion of the existence of the mind which is only contingently related to the body, the world of the senses and to other people. Bultmann's understanding of the self's relationship to God reflects this perception of the human subject. In particular, Moltmann argues that his discrimination between an authentic self-understanding and belief in a world-view (*Weltanschauung*) leads to the separation of the individual from the historical and social world. Consequently, the cause–effect nexus of science and history is not the sphere in which the individual encounters God and realizes his or her true identity.[38]

In a similar context, Moltmann criticizes Bultmann's reworking of biblical eschatology. His emphasis upon the eschatological moment which becomes the time of decisive encounter between God and the believer results in a loss of the historical and futurist dimension of Christian hope. The idea that the eschaton is the fulfilment of world history in which we are each involved is absent in Bultmann; his hermeneutical strategy has purged the New Testament of these elements. As a consequence of this he fails to appreciate the context of all human existence in the created order. As a creature, my identity is bound up with the history of other creatures and of the creation itself.

> The creature itself is a 'wayfarer', and the *homo viator* is engaged along with reality in a history that is open towards the future. Thus he does not find himself 'in the air', 'between God and the world', but he finds himself along with the world in that process to which the way is opened by the eschatological promise of Christ. It is not possible to speak of believing existence in hope and in radical openness, and at the same time consider the 'world' to be a mechanism or self-contained system of cause and effect in objective antithesis to man. Hope then fades away to the hope of the solitary soul in the prison of a petrified world, and becomes the expression of a gnostic longing for redemption.[39]

Moltmann goes on to argue that Bultmann's theology of the resurrection reinforces the individualism of his thought. The tendency to reduce the significance of the resurrection to the rise of faith in the believer rips the event out of its biblical context. The resurrection is first and foremost an event for Jesus which leaves its marks in space and time. Its context lies in Jewish hopes about the destiny of the creation, the resurrection of the dead, and the future of all humanity. To abstract the theology of the resurrection from this context is inevitably to yield to an other-worldly religion in which society and the creation are of second-order importance.[40]

Similar exegetical and theological criticisms of Bultmann can be found in Käsemann and Barth. We have already noted, in Chapter 5, the manner in which Käsemann challenges Bultmann's interpretation of Paul, and this reflects the theological criticism that Bultmann has isolated the human subject from its essential links with nature and society. Barth's perception of the Christian life has a sharper political focus due to the fact that his presentation of the work of Christ and the call of the Holy Spirit is determined by the doctrines of election and creation. The redemption and vocation of the Christian are set within the overarching purposes of God for humanity. The election of all people in Christ determines the creation, and the Christian life must be understood in terms of its acknowledgement and participation in this wider goal.

> The man in whom Christ lives, and who lives in Christ, has no option but to confirm in his action the living relationship in which God and the world are held together in the work of Christ, the self-determination of all men for God. These together and in their totality, identical with the person and work of Jesus Christ, are called in the New Testament the kingdom of God, the gracious and saving establishment of the lordship of the holy, merciful and almighty God in His creation. This kingdom alone can be the principle which controls the structure of the existence of the Christian.[41]

In her discussion of Bultmann's theology, Dorothee Sölle argues that the proper development of his existentialism lies in the direction of a more explicitly political theology. With its emphasis upon the setting of the individual in the particular and concrete circumstances of existence, Bultmann's theology requires us to pay greater heed to the social forces which govern individual life. Human existence is, to a large extent, determined by biological, economic and political forces, and if theology is to do justice to the particularity of human existence it must pay greater heed to this context. Sölle accuses Bultmann of an 'individualistic constriction' in his understanding of human existence.

> Existentialist interpretation neglects the conditions of its own preunderstanding. It grounds itself in the experience of the eschatological moment, which transcends all conditions. In its fascination with this unworldly moment, existentialist interpretation fails to consider the stamp left upon man by his past, by his origin and place; thus it overlooks the bondage arising from the fact that we come from a definite history.[42]

144

(It is, of course, no coincidence that Heidegger's philosophy has been subjected to similar criticism. Despite his insistence upon the historicality (*Geschichtlichkeit*) of human existence, Heidegger seems to locate the essence of this historicality under and within the particular circumstances of history as they are perceived by historical and social science. It is by understanding the existence underlying past history that the authentic possibilities of *Dasein* are uncovered. This search for the essence of *Dasein* within history leads to a devaluing of the particular movements, changes and forces at work in that same history. The twin possibilities confronting human beings of either owning or disowning their existence seem to remain constant and to be the transcendental conditions determining all history. For this reason, Heidegger's philosophy has been accused of displaying an ahistorical and apolitical dimension.[43])

In responding to these criticisms, Bultmann has sought to defend himself against the charge that his theology is apolitical. In his correspondence with Dorothee Sölle, he claims that the need to confess Christ amidst the particular circumstances of individual life inevitably entails a Christian obligation to become involved in social and political affairs. The inner freedom of the Christian is not a distraction from this but provides the means and motivation for such involvement.[44] At the same time, Bultmann warns against the dangers of political theology. There must be no confusion between the word of God and any particular political programme.[45] The Christian has a responsibility to make political judgements, but these particular judgements cannot themselves be identified with the message of the gospel.[46] Bultmann's theology at its best can be seen as an attempt to express the significance of the individual's relationship before God. To miss this significance is to lose an essential feature of the teaching of Jesus and the New Testament. To ignore the importance of the individual who is free and responsible before the word of God is to run the risk of yielding to a form of theological collectivism.

It is clear both from his insistence upon the historic nature of human existence and from the connection he emphasized between the indicatives of faith and the imperatives of Christian action that Bultmann was not advocating an other-worldly, private religion. Christians are called upon to confess and to enact the faith in the time and place in which they find themselves. For Bultmann himself, that entailed becoming a member of the Confessing Church in 1934. Yet despite this, there remain certain misgivings about the shape of his theology.

The tendency to set the individual alone before God is valid insofar as it asserts the value of each person in the sight of God, and the importance of responsible choice on the part of the individual. If, however, the individual is abstracted from those relationships to nature and society which shape our identity, there is a danger that the political dimension of human existence will be lost sight of. My personal identity cannot be described independently of the social situation in which I find myself and to which I ineluctably contribute. Bultmann's recognition of the moral significance of other people may be appropriate to the way in which I relate to my direct acquaintances, but my identity is determined by more than the personal encounters in which I am daily involved. It is not that the emphasis upon the significance of the human individual is misplaced. It is rather that his conception of what it is to be human is too restrictive; a more relational understanding of human existence is called for.

> Our 'neighbour' comes on the scene only in personal encounter, but not in his social reality. It is the man within arm's length or at our door who is our neighbour, but not man as he appears in the social and juridical order, in questions of aid to under-developed countries and race relationships, in social callings, roles and claims.[47]

Despite his best intentions, the initial setting of Bultmann's theology has abstracted from the reality of the human situation. The contextual and relational nature of all human existence is lost sight of in the encounter with the word of God. As a result, the physical and social dimension of life is always likely to appear as something of second-order importance from a theological perspective. Even worse, it may result in a concealed quietism which tacitly accepts the status quo. The insistence upon the centrality of a divine–human encounter which prescinds from every political context may reinforce the legitimacy of those circumstances in which that encounter takes place.[48] Recent liberation theologies have effectively analysed the concealed political assumptions that govern the form and content of all theology, and it is difficult to avoid the conclusion that Bultmann was insufficiently critical of the assumptions that underlay his own hermeneutic.[49]

Conclusion

Unlike Barth, Bultmann does not have a school of recognizable followers at the end of the twentieth century. This is largely on account of the four areas of critical dissatisfaction which we have explored in this final chapter. These criticisms, however, should not prevent us from appreciating the way in which many of his proposals have been revised and developed by recent theology and biblical scholarship. If his solutions do not satisfy, there is still much to be learned from studying them and from identifying the problems that he was responding to. His work remains important and continues to repay careful study, and his reputation will surely remain as one of the leading theologians and New Testament scholars of the twentieth century.

In our discussion of his thought we have traversed most of the contours in modern theology. It is a measure of the richness and scope of his writings that they draw together the central questions of twentieth-century theology. His life's work was grounded in a dual commitment to the witness of the Church and to the importance of honest, scientific enquiry. If we fail to appreciate that Christian faith and intellectual criticism were for him harmonious pursuits we shall not understand his theology. If we cannot follow many of his conclusions, we can do no better than pursue his intention of faithfully representing the word given to the Church while simultaneously relating it to the questions and insights of the world around us.

As a preacher, theologian, biblical critic and teacher, Bultmann's days were spent interpreting the Christian faith for the modern world. His thought, in all its richness and complexity, remains profoundly simple in its overriding intention to witness to the crucifixion of Jesus of Nazareth. Whatever controversies his writings may have created, there can be no questioning their integrity as Christian theology. These words, written in 1924, reflect his lifelong witness:

> The subject of theology is *God*, and . . . has as its content only the 'word of the cross'.[50]

Notes

1 *Church Dogmatics* III/2, ed. G.W. Bromiley and T.F. Torrance (Edinburgh, 1960), p. 446. Another significant theological critique of

Bultmann's treatment of religious language is Gerhard Ebeling's 'Zum Verständnis von R. Bultmanns Aufsatz: "Welchen Sinn hat es, von Gott zu reden?"', *Wort und Glaube* II (Tübingen, 1969), pp. 343-71. Ebeling argues that, despite his best intentions, Bultmann is in danger of identifying God with human existence. As a consequence, it becomes hard to see how we can speak of God as the subject of referential expressions.

2 *Church Dogmatics* I/2, ed. Bromiley and Torrance (Edinburgh, 1956), p. 7.

3 'Subjective revelation can consist only in the fact that objective revelation, the one truth which cannot be added to or bypassed, comes to man and is recognised and acknowledged by man. And that is the work of the Holy Spirit': ibid., p. 239.

4 E. Jüngel, *Glauben und Verstehen* (Heidelberg, 1985), p. 78.

5 Cf. 'The word of God and faith' in *Church Dogmatics* I/1, ed. Bromiley and Torrance (Edinburgh, 1956), pp. 227-47.

6 Ibid., p. 301. Cf. The correspondence between Bultmann and Barth in June 1928, following the publication of *Die Christliche Dogmatik*. Bultmann criticizes Barth for becoming enslaved to an obsolete conceptuality. Barth responds that the theologian may have to make use of a wide variety of concepts in order that the message of the Bible be clearly heard. *Letters*, pp. 38-43.

7 Barth's theology constitutes much of the background to the 'post-liberal' theology which has recently emerged in America. Here the emphasis upon the narratives of Scripture, as constituting a world of meaning which shapes Christian belief, value and practice, reflects Barth's sensitivity to the importance of Christian dogma. Cf. Hans Frei, *The Eclipse of Biblical Narrative* (New Haven, 1974); George Lindbeck, *The Nature of Doctrine* (London, 1984); William Placher, *Unapologetic Theology* (Louisville, 1989).

8 E.g. *Myth and Reality* (London, 1964), ch. 1, pp. 1-20.

9 *Myths, Models, and Paradigms* (London, 1974), pp. 26ff.

10 Ibid., p. 27. Cf. Paul Ricoeur, 'Preface to Bultmann' in *The Conflict of Interpretations* (Evanston, 1974), pp. 381-401; and my own 'Meaning, truth and realism in Bultmann and Lindbeck', *Religious Studies* 26 (1990), pp. 183-98.

11 *Christ Without Myth* (London, 1962), p. 172.

12 Ogden has developed this more recently in *The Point of Christology* (London, 1982), pp. 127-47. For a helpful guide to process theology see David Pailin, *God and the Processes of Reality* (London, 1989).

13 Their works are available in the following translations: Ernst Käsemann, 'The problem of the historical Jesus' in *Essays on New Testament Themes* (London, 1964), pp. 15-47; Günther Bornkamm, *Jesus of Nazareth* (London, 1960); Ernst Fuchs, *Studies of the*

Historical Jesus (London, 1964); Gerhard Ebeling, *Theology and Proclamation* (London, 1966).

14 Käsemann, 'Blind alleys in the "Jesus of history" controversy' in *New Testament Questions of Today* (London, 1969), p. 46.

15 Ebeling, pp. 48ff. Pannenberg has argued in a *reductio ad absurdum* of Bultmann's position that, if the historical Jesus were of no real interest to the Christian faith, then his name would have eventually been dropped from the Christian understanding of existence: 'On historical and theological hermeneutic' in *Basic Questions in Theology* 1 (London, 1970), p. 149.

16 Ebeling, p. 64.

17 Cf. Barth, 'Rudolf Bultmann—an attempt to understand him', K & M II, p. 111; D.M. Baillie, *God Was in Christ* (London, 1948), pp. 37ff.; David Cairns, *A Gospel Without Myth* (London, 1960), pp. 136–63; Nils Dahl, 'The problem of the historical Jesus' in C.E. Braaten and R.A. Harrisville (eds), *Kerygma and History* (New York, 1962), p. 161.

18 'The problem of the historical Jesus'.

19 Ibid., pp. 37–45.

20 'Blind alleys in the "Jesus of history" controversy', p. 52.

21 James Robinson, *A New Quest of the Historical Jesus* (London, 1959), ch. 4, pp. 73–92. In the writings of Fuchs and Ebeling there is a strong emphasis upon the encounter occasioned by the words of Jesus, especially the parables. This reflects their belief in the hermeneutical significance of a language-event (*Sprachereignis*). Their approach has been described as 'the new hermeneutic' and it bears the marks of the influence of the later Heidegger. Cf. Ernst Fuchs, *Hermeneutik* (Tübingen, 1970), esp. pp. 219–30; Gerhard Ebeling, 'Word of God and hermeneutics' in *Word and Faith* (London, 1963), pp. 305–32.

22 'Das Verhältnis der urchristlichen Christusbotschaft zum historischen Jesus' (1962); 'The primitive Christian kerygma and the historical Jesus' in C.E. Braaten and R.A. Harrisville (eds), *The Historical Jesus and the Kergymatic Christ* (New York, 1964), p. 30. Cf. Van A. Harvey and Schubert Ogden, 'Wie neu ist die "Neue Frage nach dem historischen Jesus"?', *Zeitschrift für Theologie und Kirche* 59 (1962), pp. 46–87.

23 R.S. Barbour, *Traditio-Historical Criticism of the Gospels* (London, 1972), p. 33.

24 E. Jüngel, *Glauben und Verstehen*, p. 70. Cf. Peter Stuhlmacher, *Jesus von Nazareth—Christus des Glaubens* (Stuttgart, 1988), pp. 11ff.

25 For an analysis of the way in which narrative interpretation of the gospels disappeared from view after the Enlightenment see Hans Frei, *The Eclipse of Biblical Narrative*.

26 *Jesus: An Experiment in Christology* (London, 1979), p. 75f. A similar strategy can be found in J.P. Mackey, *Jesus: The Man and the Myth* (London, 1979).

27 *The Point of Christology*, p. 56.

28 Ibid., p. 57.

29 *The Historian and the Believer* (London, 1967), pp. 266ff.

30 *Church Dogmatics* I/2, Section 17, 'The revelation of God as the abolition of religion', pp. 280-361.

31 Cf. Martin Evang's analysis of Bultmann's early interest in the nature of true religion: 'Die Konzentration des jungen Rudolf Bultmann auf das Thema wahrer Religion' in *Rudolf Bultmann in seiner Frühzeit* (Tübingen, 1988), pp. 251-332.

32 Cf. John Hick, 'Jesus and the world religions' in *The Myth of God Incarnate* (London, 1977), pp. 167-85.

33 'Reply' in C.W. Kegley (ed.), *The Theology of Rudolf Bultmann* (London, 1966), p. 275. Cf. John Macquarrie, 'Philosophy and theology in Bultmann's thought', ibid., pp. 127-43.

34 *Christ Without Myth*, p. 130.

35 *The Point of Christology*, pp. 127-47.

36 'Review of Schubert Ogden, *Christ Without Myth*', *Journal of Religion* 42 (1962), p. 226.

37 *The Church in the Power of the Spirit* (London, 1977), ch. 4, pp. 133-96.

38 'The theology of the transcendental subjectivity of man' in *Theology of Hope* (London, 1967), pp. 58-69. For an analysis of the Cartesian bewitchment of theology see Fergus Kerr, *Theology After Wittgenstein* (Oxford, 1986).

39 Moltmann, ibid., p. 69.

40 Ibid., pp. 182-97.

41 *Church Dogmatics* IV/3, ed. Bromiley and Torrance (Edinburgh, 1962), pp. 598-9. Cf. Heinrich Ott, 'Der individualistische Zug im Denken Bultmanns' in *Geschichte und Heilsgeschichte in der Theologie Rudolf Bultmanns* (Tübingen, 1955), pp. 181-93.

42 *Political Theology* (Philadelphia, 1974), ch. 4, p. 45; Cf. Johannes Metz, *Theology of the World* (New York, 1969). For a discussion of Sölle's critique of Bultmann, see Christopher Rowland and Mark Corner, *Liberating Exegesis* (London, 1990), pp. 69-74.

43 Cf. Moltmann, pp. 255-61; T.W. Adorno, *The Jargon of Authenticity* (London, 1973), e.g. p. 142.

44 Letter to Dorothee Sölle cited by Antje Bultmann Lemke, 'Der unveröffentliche Nachlass von Rudolf Bultmann' in B. Jaspert (ed.), *Rudolf Bultmanns Werk und Wirkung* (Darmstadt, 1984), pp. 205f.

45 'Gedanken über die gegenwärtige theologische Situation', GV III, p. 195.

46 Ibid., p. 196. The Sölle–Bultmann discussion is analysed by Hans Hübner, *Politische Theologie und existentiale Interpretation* (Witten, 1973).

47 Moltmann, op. cit., p. 315.

48 'Bultmann should have acknowledged the fact that he was a paid officer of the state, a professor, thus an institutional participant in that political and military machine which was involved in the war of 1914–1918, not merely passively but actively. It was a professor's public duty to research, teach and examine theology. Bultmann should at least have raised one question, namely whether the official theological enterprise he was involved in might not have contributed to the collective, nonsensical crime of the war—a war among allegedly Christian nations. As historical-critical theologian, even more as a critical hermeneuticist, he could not leave out the critical assessment of the condition of his historical situation. The factual, institutional partiality of the alleged distance and neutrality of the scholar should have been a matter of critical investigation': Dieter Georgi, 'Rudolf Bultmann's *Theology of the New Testament* revisited' in E. Hobbs (ed.), *Bultmann, Retrospect and Prospect* (Philadelphia, 1985), pp. 83f.

49 For an analysis of liberation theology on this issue see J.M. Bonino, *Revolutionary Theology Comes of Age* (London, 1975), pp. 86–105; T. Witvliet, 'The epistemological break' in *A Place in the Sun* (London, 1985), pp. 24–43; Duncan Forrester, *Theology and Politics* (Oxford, 1988), ch. 3, pp. 57–82.

50 'Liberal theology and the latest theological movement', FU, p. 29.

Index